Rents, Accounts, Lent, Massage

Rents: 'A superb and touching comedy about the lives of two "rent" boys in Edinburgh.' *Time Out*

'What you would never guess about *Rents* in advance is that it is so funny. Here we are, faced with a story about youthful prostitution (male), poverty and urban paranoia . . . And yet, there it is at the Lyric Studio, Hammersmith, rolling them in the aisles. *Rents* is a play which touches on all kinds of problems, but it is not by any means a problem play . . . A wholly enjoyable experience.' *Plays and Players*

Accounts: 'Portrays the kind of world we rarely see on the British stage . . . Wilcox very skilfully counterpoints the struggle of a young widow and her two sons to make a go of their farm with the two boys' attempt to cope with their emotional problems.' *Guardian*

'A play so securely rooted and thoroughly imagined that the characters are able to take on an independent life in one's imagination . . . it is very unusual to care about the fate of characters in the theatre today because it is very unusual for them to be created with the completeness manifested in *Accounts*.' *Scotsman*

Lent: 'A finely tuned, intricately woven and beautifully acted period piece about adolescence and old age that operates like a time capsule, divulging its treasures by slow degrees.' *Time Out*

'A metaphysical play. It is based on the proposition that the rigours of Lent are followed by the joyous release of Easter. But this release has nothing to do with the resurrection of Christ. It uses a Catholic title only to illustrate a pagan thing . . . A fine and original play.' *Times Literary Supplement*

Massage: 'Startles with its compassion for two bruised egos.' *City Limits*

'Shot through with wry, extremely uncomfortable perceptions.' *Financial Times*

Michael Wilcox lives in Northumberland. His plays include *Accounts*, for which he shared the George Devine Award (Traverse Theatre, Edinburgh, and Riverside Studios, London, 1981); *Rents* (Traverse Theatre, 1979, and Lyric Theatre, Hammersmith, 1982); *Lent* (Lyric Studio, Hammersmith, 1983); *78 Revolutions* (Traverse Theatre and Lyric Studio, 1984); *Massage* (Lyric Theatre, Hammersmith, 1986); and *Green Fingers* (Live Theatre, Newcastle-upon-Tyne, and King's Head Theatre, London, 1990). He has written scripts for television and libretti for opera. He is also editor of Methuen's *Gay Plays* series.

Methuen World Classics and
Methuen Contemporary Dramatists

MICHAEL WILCOX

Plays: 1

Rents
Accounts
Lent
Massage

with an introduction by the author

Methuen Drama

METHUEN C.ONTEMPORARY DRAMATISTS

This edition first published in Great Britain 1997
by Methuen Drama

Random House UK Limited
20 Vauxhall Bridge Road, London SW1V 2SA

Random House Australia (Pty) Limited
20 Alfred Street, Milsons Point, Sydney,
New South Wales 2061, Australia

Random House New Zealand Limited
18 Poland Road, Glenfield, Auckland 10, New Zealand

Random House South Africa (Pty) Limited
Endulini, 5a Jubilee Road, Parktown 2193, South Africa

Random House UK Limited Reg. No. 954009

Rents was first published in 1983 by Methuen London as a Methuen New
Theatrescript. Copyright © 1983, 1997 by Michael Wilcox
Accounts was first published in 1984 by Methuen London in a volume entitled
Gay Plays. Copyright © 1984, 1997 by Michael Wilcox
Lent was first published in 1983 by Methuen London as a Methuen New
Theatrescript. Copyright © 1983, 1997 by Michael Wilcox
Massage was first published in 1987 by Methuen London as a Methuen New
Theatrescript. Copyright © 1987, 1997 by Michael Wilcox

Copyright in this collection © 1997 by Michael Wilcox
Copyright in the Introduction © 1997 by Michael Wilcox
The author has asserted his moral rights

ISBN 0-413-71110-2

A CIP catalogue record for this book
is available from the British Library

Typeset by Wilmaset Ltd, Birkenhead, Wirral
Printed and bound in Great Britain by Cox & Wyman Ltd, Reading, Berks

Caution

Contents

Michael Wilcox:
Chronology

1974   Abandons teaching career to become a full-time
        playwright
        Dekka and Dava (pub. Methuen, 1987)
        The Boy Who Cried Stop! (Stagecoach, Tyneside
        Theatre Company)

1975   *Grimm Tales* (Stagecoach, Tyneside Theatre
        Company)
        The Atom Bomb Project (Stagecoach, Tyneside
        Theatre Company)
        Roar Like Spears (Alabama Drama Institute,
        Montevallo, USA)

1976   *Standard Procedure* (Afternoon Theatre, BBC Radio;
        pub. Iron Press, 1978)

1977–8 Resident playwright at the Dovecot Arts Centre,
        Stockton-on-Tees
        The Blacketts of Bright Street (Dovecot Arts Centre)
        Mowgli (Dovecot Arts Centre)
        Pioneers (Dovecot Arts Centre)
        Phantom of the Fells (Live Theatre Company,
        Newcastle upon Tyne)

1979   *Rents* (Traverse Theatre, Edinburgh)

1980   Thames Television Award
        Resident playwright at the Traverse Theatre

1981   *Accounts* (Traverse Theatre and Riverside Studios,
        London; joint winner of the George Devine Award,
        shared with Hanif Kureishi)
        Clean Sweep (STV)
        Cricket (Plays for Tomorrow, BBC TV)

1982   *Accounts* filmed for Channel Four's Film on Four
        Midnight Feast (STV)
        Accounts (Monday Play, BBC Radio)

1983   *Lent* (Lyric Studio, Hammersmith)
        American premiere of *Accounts* (Hudson Guild
        Theater, New York)
        Voted Most Promising Playwright by the British
        Theatre Association
        In Disgrace (STV)
        Burnt Futures (*Crown Court*, Granada TV)

1984   *78 Revolutions* (Traverse Theatre and Lyric Studio,
        Hammersmith)
        Lent filmed for BBC TV's Screen Two
        A Party to Crime (*A Case for Justice*, Granada TV:
        entire series recorded, but never televised for
        political reasons)
        Edited *Gay Plays: 1* (pub. Methuen)

1985   *Rents* tour of Australia
        Lent wins Pye Television Award for Best TV Script
        1984–5, TRICS Award for Best Single Play, and
        TRICS Best Actor Award for Harry Andrews

1986   *Massage* (Lyric Studio, Hammersmith)
        Edited *Gay Plays: 2* (pub. Methuen)

1987   Berlin premiere of *Massage* (Junges Theater)

1988   *Inspector Morse: Last Bus to Woodstock* (Zenith for
        Central Television)
        Edited *Gay Plays: 3* (pub. Methuen)

1989   Series of five training films for the British Medical
        Association

1990   *Tornrak* (librettist for composer John Metcalf;
        Welsh National Opera)
        Edited *Gay Plays: 4* (pub. Methuen)
        Green Fingers (Northern Stage and Live Theatre;
        winner of the Second Stage Competition, leading

to new production at the King's Head Theatre, London)

1991   Autobiography: *Outlaw in the Hills: A Writer's Year* (pub. Methuen)

1992   *Winning the Peace: Doctor Finlay* (STV)
Time Windows (Palace Theatre, Westcliff-on-Sea)

1993   *Stolen Lives: Doctor Finlay* (in collaboration with Simon Donald; STV)
Cullercoats Tommy (librettist for composer Eddie McGuire; Northern Stage, Northern Sinfonia and Dance City)
Lent (Saturday Night Theatre, BBC Radio)

1994   New version of *Time Windows* (NTC Touring Company)
Edited *Gay Plays: 5* (pub. Methuen)

1995   *The Reluctant King* (new libretto for Chabrier's opera, *Le Roi malgre lui*, in collaboration with Jeremy Sams; Opera North)

1997   *Benjamin Britten and Vicious Society* (pub. Absolute Press)

Introduction

Here are two pairs of plays. *Accounts* was written as the rural
counterpart of the urban *Rents*, and *Massage* complements
Lent. *Rents* was written in Edinburgh and Newcastle in 1976.
That's before we had heard of Aids and at a time when
Scottish law had not caught up with English law as far as
homosexuality was concerned. In Scotland, all homosexual
acts between males of any age and in any circumstances
were criminal offences with the ultimate threat of life
imprisonment for those found guilty. Oddly, homosexual
acts between women were not criminalised at all, as though
the law regarded women as some sort of sub-species not
worthy of homophobic legislation. Obviously, male
homosexuals had to have some sort of life north of the Border
and there was an active gay subculture involving bars and
discos as well as campaigning and social groups. The best
known of these in the '70s was the Scottish Minorities Group
(SMG), whose curious title deliberately excluded the
criminal implications of the word 'homosexual'. In 1976,
like Richard Ridley in *Rents*, I found myself standing in at an
Edinburgh college for a few weeks while one of the lecturers
was busy with other duties. As in the play, I was introduced
to Edinburgh's gay and criminal underworld by one of the
students. Before going to bed each night, I wrote a short play
featuring aspects of what I'd learnt earlier. The following
morning, the drama students in my group, including Jimmy
Chisholm who was to play Robert at the Traverse three
years later, would read and discuss the latest script. At the
end of two weeks, there was a substantial pile of short plays
that was given the collective title of *Rents*, from which the
final Traverse script was drafted.

This spontaneous and practical method of writing, as well
as providing an unusual experience for my eager and

mischievous students, was similar to the working method that I had used throughout my two-year-old writing career. I had been living off my wits, based in a busy bed-sit in Jesmond, Newcastle upon Tyne. Almost everything I owned was crammed into one small room. I had written short plays for youth theatre groups, the Tyneside Theatre Company's TIE (Theatre in Education) 'Stagecoach' company, and had the invaluable experience of working at the excellent Alabama Drama Institute, based at Montevallo, USA. Almost everything I had written was to order, with one group or other in mind, and received at least a handful of performances, generally in non-theatre venues. I was selling short plays for ten pounds each to pay the rent. Just as important, I was beginning to learn my trade.

The character of Richard Ridley was a caricature of myself as I might become in fifteen years if I didn't watch out, solitary and dull, inclined to selfishness, and sufficiently battered by experience not to open the door too wide to the Roberts of this world. I had left a successful teaching career in 1974, and in that year finally came out to myself as gay. Explorations of Edinburgh's gay underworld were novel to me, in my virginal innocence, and *Rents* was to prove the ultimate 'coming out' experience. As far as that projection of myself was concerned, mercifully, a better fate awaited me, welcoming many Roberts into my life, none of whom ripped me off, although, like Richard, I remain to this day a passionate collector of classical vinyl.

During the '70s, I was influenced greatly by the Northumbrian-based Scottish playwright, C. P. Taylor. Cecil was regularly produced at the Traverse at that time and I often drove him up to rehearsals, which I was then able to observe. Cecil, whose sudden death shocked all who knew and loved him, was the tireless benefactor of every writer who contacted him, and it was he who drew artistic director Chris Parr's attention to *Rents*. My provincial career changed overnight with the 1979 premiere and it remains the most performed of all my plays.

I always thought *Rents* was about money and survival rather than homosexuality, and when the Traverse, where I became writer-in-residence in 1980, asked for a new play, I decided to explore similar themes in a rural context. Living in a small cottage at the northern end of the Pennines not far from Hadrian's Wall, I was in the middle of a farming community. The Young Farmers' Club, which in my part of the world does not suffer from the social exclusivity that can exist elsewhere, perform either a play or an entertainment each year for a national competition. I was recruited to provide a script for the Haltwhistle YFC and decided to write a short play set on an 'out-by' (extremely remote) farm. The result was the first draft of the jelly-throwing scene that concludes Act One of *Accounts*. For the Traverse commission, I developed this material into a full-length play, mirroring the *Rents* casting by featuring two teenage boys trying to run a newly purchased farm after the death of their father. The older male interloper this time is a chartered surveyor with accounting skills and his name, James Ridley-Bowes, deliberately echoes that of Richard Ridley in the earlier play. Unlike Richard, James is unwilling to acknowledge his homosexuality, believing that devoting his life to young rugby players and dating Donald in no way compromises his superficial straightness. What he hasn't realised is that his young rugby star is gay himself and isn't going to let his life slip by without doing something positive about it. Donald also has an intense and sometimes violent relationship with his older brother, with whom he has always shared a bed, and when it becomes clear that their sexual lives are moving apart irreconcilably, the possibility of extreme violence is frighteningly real. Sadly, shotgun tragedies in the form of accidents, suicides and even murder are far from unknown in rural communities, and my play could, reasonably, have ended in disaster.

The lads may seem very young to undertake so much professional responsibility, but that's the way things are in the country. As soon as they could walk, the boys would have had the hens to feed and orphaned lambs to care for. The additional complications of being part of the European Common Market, which in my story actually saves their necks, has lost none of its topicality nearly two decades later.

With hindsight, one can see that even though the Mawsons slaughtered their dairy herd, they would now be facing an even bigger crisis in the shape of BSE, while Donald's case for diversifying the family resources to exploit tourism now looks like common sense. I would guess that Mary never remarried but runs the camp site on the Burn Pastures, that Andy lives with his wife and two children in the detached cottage that now stands on the site of the milking parlour, and that Donald is still with his mother, although he enjoys a long-term and secret relationship with a married barrister in Kelso. He represented the South of Scotland at rugby football as a speedy winger and plays regularly for 'Tweed'.

The success of the two Traverse plays aroused interest in my work from commercial managements. *Lent* was commissioned by Michael Codron, although, in the event, he decided not to produce it. It was written in two weeks and, unusually for me, the final version contains about 95 per cent of the first draft. It is the most autobiographical of all my plays. My family has owned Alleyn Court Preparatory School in Essex since 1904 and like Paul Blake I lived all the year round in the school. In real life, I have two brothers and a sister and my mother is very much alive as I write this. However, my father did die when I was nine and there were prototypes, who were 'gathered in' long ago, as Mrs Blake would have said, for all the characters in the play. *Lent* is, however, entirely a work of fiction and I have transferred the location of the school to Berkshire and made Gorse Park a distinctly Edwardian boarding school, whereas Alleyn Court in 1956 was predominantly a day school with more than 200 pupils of whom only about 50 were boarders.

Among other things, I wanted to put a young boy centre stage for two hours in an adult play. We underestimate constantly what young people are able to achieve and I had no doubts that casting the play as it was written was entirely practical, but to this day there has never been a single professional production using a boy actor. The film version that was included in BBC TV's first Screen Two series came the nearest so far to present my stage play as originally intended, and there have been a number of distinguished amateur productions using boy actors, as well as an excellent BBC Radio 'Saturday Night Theatre' version. But the lack of an authentic theatrical professional production remains the biggest disappointment of my career so far.

Young Paul is fighting for his survival in the confines of an enclosed environment ruled by old people from a bygone age. Not only has he lost his parents, but he has become little more than a boarder in what was once his own home. His tough old grandmother has a keen sense of fair play but is incapable of affection, while the newly promoted Mr Edwards and his dangerously batty wife are cruel and deceitful bullies. Their treatment of the displaced Paul amounts to abuse by humiliation. They would indeed take delight in 'cracking his shell' if they could. Only old Matey provides Paul with sane company and affectionate support. Just occasionally he provides Paul with glimpses of the dark world that he has managed so successfully to conceal. Matey loves boys. His marriage was an immediate disaster. If he and Paul were of similar ages, they might indeed have become lovers and travelled 'to the ends of the earth and back again!' Paul, who shaves his pubic hair 'with Daddy's razor' and who has no desire to become a man, uses what power he possesses to ensure that Matey has a home for the rest of his life. For his part, Matey explains to Paul that 'there's too much mud . . . that's frightened to be disturbed' and begs Paul to let him live out his few remaining years in peace. To me, this is a beautiful and profound relationship in which a mutual love, which has a scarcely concealed sexual dimension, expresses itself with caring self-denial.

The three characters we meet in *Massage* are all, by contrast, abusive. If Paul Blake is hungry for knowledge of what his post-Edwardian world fussily refers to as 'the facts of life', young Rikki has been only too aware of the relationship between sex and survival from far too early an age. *Massage* isn't a play about gay people. In fact, all the characters are heterosexual. But for one reason or another, their lives are such a mess that they live off each other like sexual cannibals. Even Simon, who we never see, appears to be just as exploitative. The duplicitous Dodge, whose every word we learn to doubt by the end of the play, conducts a vigorous defence of what he claims happened between him and the pre-pubescent Simon, leading some to feel that the play itself is an apologia for paedophilia. It was never intended to be and I hardly think that is a sustainable interpretation. But neither do I think of Dodge as purely evil. If his description of what happened between himself and Simon on that camping holiday is more or less the truth, something happened that shouldn't have done, even if it was Simon himself who instigated the seduction. Nevertheless, in a sane world, the experience might have been simply a curious twist in growing up rather than a major disaster, as far as Simon is concerned. But the long-term effect on Dodge, with his secret hoard of child pornography and his desperate decision to phone an escort agency to find a surrogate Simon, marks him out as someone in urgent need of help.

Whether his tumultuous contact with Rikki, with its games, challenges and betrayals, is destined to be part of the healing process or a compounding of his problems, we can only guess. And Heaven knows what happens when Simon's self-righteous mother returns home to find out what her mischievous son is up to next. The fact that this single-scene play doesn't allow us to find out may be tantalising to some, or a blessed relief to others.

Massage was easily the most difficult play to write of those in this anthology, both technically, because of its real-time structure, and because of its disturbing subject matter. Whilst the other plays have been tweaked and, I hope, clarified, there has been wholesale rewriting of *Massage* with a cynical new ending.

Michael Wilcox
November 1996

Rents

Rents was first produced, in this five actor version, by the Traverse Theatre Company during the 1979 Edinburgh International Festival. The cast was as follows:

Phil MacFerson	David Bannerman
Robert	Jimmy Chisholm
Richard Ridley	David Whitaker
Eddie	Campbell Morrison
Albert, *the accountant*	
Peter, *the solicitor*	
Spider	Carey Wilson
Thomas, *from Harpenden*	
Mr MacFerson	

Directed by Chris Parr
Designed by Adrian Mudd
Lighting by David Horn
Sound by Matt McKenzie

For the revival at the Lyric Studio, Hammersmith, from 17 April to 8 May 1982, **Richard Ridley** was played by Jonathon Newth

Rents was again presented at the Lyric Theatre, Hammersmith, from 2 February to 10 March 1984, with the following cast:

Phil MacFerson	Stevan Rimkus
Robert	Douglas Sannachan
Richard Ridley	Paul Jesson
Eddie	Kenny Ireland
Albert, *the accountant*	
Peter, *the solicitor*	
Spider	Robert McIntosh
Thomas, *from Harpenden*	
Mr MacFerson	

Directed by William Gaskill
Designed by Dermot Hayes
Lighting designed by Andy Phillips
Sound by Matt McKenzie

Act One

Edinburgh in the late 70s.

Phil *is naked at his apartment off the Dalry Road.*

Phil I need a man . . . a real man. Oh Scotland . . . where has your virility trickled? What I want is a worker, hot from the production line . . . with a day's sweat on him. Body odours really excite me . . . saltiness mingled with fragrant machine oil. I need a Scot, bright-eyed from an oil rig . . . a boiler maker . . . a crofter from the Outer Hebrides. The best I've done this week was Malcolm from the Golden Wonder factory.

Robert *at the apartment.*

Robert I came on the scene when I was fifteen, travelling in to Edinburgh from Livingstone at weekends. I was astonished at the sort of custom I had . . . all these men coming all over me in the most unlikely situations. If a guy took me to the cinema I'd let him screw me in the bog while the other kids were queuing for ice creams. I couldn't stop myself. I just loved to see a grown man get that excited about me . . . my body . . . God . . . my body . . . and feeling the tension . . . and sweat of him when he came . . . and his dejection as he cleaned himself up afterwards. One guy punched me in the mouth when I laughed at him. I went with him again . . .

Eddie *on the streets of Edinburgh.*

Eddie I first met Phil MacFerson in Rose Street . . . just along from the Kenilworth. This was a couple of years ago. He just came up to me from nowhere and started talking. I can't remember what he said . . . but we ended up going for a drink. And only after about half an hour did we realise that it was his mother that was going with my Norma! Well . . . she was mine. I mean . . . we were together and getting by. It wasn't all . . . oh . . . never mind. But not content with one half of his bloody family taking off with my Norma, here's this bent bastard chatting me up . . . *me*! I never realised what he was after . . . not at first. He never said anything . . . but it just dawned on me . . . slowly. I never went with him. *I didn't.*

Richard *is preparing to leave his house in Newcastle 130 miles south of Edinburgh, across the border in England. The record that is playing is the second movement of Mozart's Divertimento KV 138 (The Italian Quartet).*

Richard   I've been up since half past five. It's been one of those special mornings when the sun wakes you up and you really don't want to stay in bed a second longer. I was tempted to do some work in the garden, but drank a pot of tea instead.

Music sounds so good this morning. This is part of a Mozart Divertimento played by the Italian Quartet . . .

No one in their right mind would leave home on a day like this. I've got to stand in for this lecturer at Charles Stuart College up in Edinburgh. Just for a few weeks. It's extra cash, I suppose. Makes a change from Newcastle Poly . . . There isn't a decent record shop in Edinburgh. They sell everything at full price, even the boxed sets. If you're going to buy something, you might as well pay as little as possible. Edinburgh's full-price city.

The apartment of **Phil** *and* **Robert** *in Edinburgh, off the Dalry Road. It's just after eight o'clock in the morning.* **Robert** *has dashed across the road to the supermarket, that opens at eight, to fetch provisions. He arrives back a few minutes later.*

Phil   Success?

Robert   Of course!

Robert *puts down a carrier bag with a few groceries in it.* **Phil** *looks through it, unimpressed.*

Phil Tea and a packet of biscuits!

Robert You've got to pay for something.

Robert *has various articles hidden all over him after his shop-lifting raid. He produces them one by one, and throws them across to* **Phil**.

Robert Coffee ... beans ... steak and kidney pies ... three! Beans ... salad cream ... beans ... Whiskers.

Phil We haven't got a cat!

Robert Don't be fussy! Beans ... tin of carrots ... mushy peas ... beans ... a Kit-Kat ...

Phil Only one?

Robert Beans ...

Phil We've got over two hundred cans of beans in the cupboard. Can you not resist pinching beans for a month or two?

Robert They're on special offer this week.

Phil What's wrong with sardines?

Robert Hold on! Sardines ... sardines ... sardines ... and sardines ... and beans ...

Phil Terrific!

Robert Aren't you pleased?

Phil What am I doing in college, Robert?

Robert What am I doing in a run-down men's shop? The new jeans are in.

Phil I want a pair.

Robert Which side are you hanging this season?

Phil I haven't got any money.

Robert Stand up ... prominent leftist ...

Phil Are they tailored?

Robert   No ... but every time a man comes into the shop I reach for my tape measure. I'm Edinburgh's leading authority on inside legs.

Phil   I'm 30–31 ... I want a pair.

Robert   Why do you always plead like a little child when you want something? Stop pleading.

Phil   We'll nick 'em ... this morning.

Robert   No way.

Phil   Yes.

Robert   She watches me like a hawk ... no.

Phil   Yes.

Robert   How?

Phil   Put two pairs of jeans – size 30–31 ... onto one coat hanger ... right? Then I'll come in with a bag ... some other shopping ... don't recognise me ... you mustn't recognise me ...

Robert   I said no ...

Phil   ... and then come and measure me ... no, serve me!

Robert   I'm not going to.

Phil   ... give me the hanger with the two jeans on ... I'll try them on ...

Robert   We have stalls with swing doors ... like a Western saloon ...

Phil   I'll put one pair in my bag ... and try on the other pair.

Robert   They can see everything ...

Phil   ... then I'll decide not to buy ... and give the jeans back ... and away ... done it ... we've done it! The perfect crime ... true genius for you.

Robert   What do I do with the empty coat hanger?

Phil   Easy ... lose it ...

Robert   Lose it ...

Phil   Yes.

Robert   I'll shit myself.

Phil   You won't.

Robert   I will.

Phil   You hate her . . . think how much you hate her,
Robert . . . how much does she pay you an hour?

Robert   I don't know.

Phil   How much?

Robert   About 60 pence.

Phil   Robbery! She's making a fortune out of you. How can
you rent yourself out for 60 pence an hour? Is that all you're
worth? That bitch has corrupted your sense of values. She's
ripped you off so much she owes us jeans . . . cords . . .
Wrangler shirts . . . Oh Robert . . . we must do this thing
together.

Robert   I'll see.

Phil   I'll be in at ten o'clock precisely.

Robert   What do I get out of it?

Richard *at college.*

Richard   Now I've just been told . . . twenty minutes
ago . . . that I'm going to be lecturing you on the following
plays. *Everyman* in the edition by A. C. Cawley . . . *Henry IV
Part One* . . . and just to confuse you totally . . . *Henry IV* by
Pirandello . . . We'll be using Eric Bentley's edition. There's a
set of those in the bookroom. The *Everyman*s are being used by
another group and photocopies will be available later in the
week.

Now . . . you may be wondering . . . as I am . . . what these
three plays have in common . . . why they've been lumped
together. Unlikely bedfellows . . .

(*Aside.*) The buggers at this place don't waste much time. I'm
shoved in to lecture on *Everyman* at half an hour's notice.
Thank God the students haven't read it either . . .

So the Messenger tells the audience right at the start that life is
transitory . . . we're just passing through life and that
judgement awaits us. Nothing lasts. And that *that* knowledge
should guide our moral conduct. Now I'd like you to
consider . . . er . . . well . . . if you don't believe in God . . . or at
least . . . in Divine Judgement . . . whether the purpose of
Everyman . . . which the messenger points out to us . . . has
any moral force. We may believe that at our death, the light is
just switched out forever . . . and that's that. And if our
conduct during life is not to be regulated by fear of what might
come to us after death, why not just live for the excitement . . .
the passion . . . the fleshliness . . . of life . . . and to hell with
repressive, false morality?

(*Aside.*) They seem to believe every word I say! Half the girls
are scribbling away as though I've just stepped down from
Mount Parnassus.

Richard *sees a face pressed up against the window in the door. It's*
Phil.

Richard   In the middle of my lecture a face is pressed
against the window in the door . . . staring . . . like a challenge.
There he is again, lurking by the toilets . . .

Phil   Richard . . .

Richard   What? Oh . . .

Phil   Are you going for lunch?

Richard   Where is it? I'm lost in this place.

Phil   Take these . . . I'll show you.

Phil *hands him luncheon vouchers.*

Richard   Oh . . .

Phil   Lunch vouchers . . . just hand them over to the woman
at the till . . . lunches aren't bad. I've got plenty . . . don't
worry . . . Do you play pool?

Richard   Yes.

Phil   We'll have a game after lunch. You're from
Newcastle.

Richard Aye...

Phil I was down there a few weeks ago... at the Casablanca...

Richard You naughty boy.

Phil Will you come to a film tonight? I want you to come, Richard... come and see *Fox* with me... you must come and see it with me. I don't want to go alone... none of my friends... none of them will come... I don't want to go alone... I want you to come with me. I want to talk to you, Richard... Richard, I think you're someone I can talk to... I'm going home after lunch... we could meet...

Richard What's your name again?

Phil Phil... just call me Phil... I don't like Philip... you needn't pay me in or anything... I'll pay for us both if you want... come with me to see *Fox*...

Richard Let's go and have some lunch.

Phil Will you help me, Richard? I'm doing Vladimir for my assessment. The first seven pages of *Waiting for Godot*. I don't understand it. Will you help me, Richard?

Richard I'm hungry.

Phil It's this way. Do you like my new jeans?

They go.

Robert *is working in the men's shop.* **Eddie** *enters.*

Robert Look at the state of that!

Eddie What's your name?

Robert What?

Eddie Why are you staring at me?

Robert What?

Eddie Why do you keep staring down below my waist?

Robert I'm not staring at you.

Eddie Are you trying to start an argument?

Robert   No. Do you want anything?

Eddie   I'd love to suck you off.

Robert   Ahhh . . . get out of this shop . . . I'll call the police . . .

Eddie   Do you sell studded belts?

Robert   No we don't . . . now please leave at once.

Eddie   You're looking at me as though I was a poof or something . . .

Robert   I was not.

Eddie   I know how to deal with queers.

Robert   Out!

Eddie   I'll follow you home. I know you live with Phil MacFerson.

Robert   Jesus Christ . . .

Eddie   See you around . . .

Eddie *leaves.*

Richard *back at the college.*

Richard   . . . so I've agreed to meet Phil outside the cinema at 7.15 this evening. I didn't tell him I'd already seen *Fox* as part of a Fassbinder season at the Tyneside Film Theatre. I didn't like the film much anyway . . . two hours of homosexual misery. Who wants to pay money for that sort of shit? But I do want to watch Phil watching it . . . and I am on some sort of holiday. But now I'm going to take a trip round the record shops.

Eddie *is following* **Robert** *after work.*

Eddie   . . . you see Edinburgh's falling apart and I don't want to fall apart with it. Someone's got to make a stand and I'm not frightened of turning over a few stones. Your hands are bound to get dirty in a place like this. MacFerson's dirt. He has this habit of turning up and worming his way into

people's lives. You know . . . like assaulting your space . . .
indecently. And that bastard is free to walk around the
streets. I've been out getting a new job today. Plenty of jobs in
Edinburgh. There is no unemployment problem in this city. I
could have got a job weeding in the botanical gardens . . .
turned it down . . . took a job as a chef in The Golden Egg. I
wanted a job with a uniform.

Back at **Phil**'s *apartment.* **Phil** *is with* **Albert**, *an accountant.*

Phil   Have a coffee before you go, Albert?

Albert   No thanks, dear boy . . . I don't drink much coffee
these days. It's partly the caffeine . . . keeps me awake . . . even
in the afternoon. Gives me indigestion too . . . ulcers . . .
always been a bit of a problem. Do you suffer?

Phil   Not yet.

Albert   No. Too young. I blame them on calculators
actually. Dreadful things. Have you got one?

Phil   No.

Albert   Ohhh . . . I'll give you one for Christmas. I've
always had a good head for figures . . . which . . . you will
agree . . . is a help in my profession. I was slow and steady and
got there in the end . . . as with other things, dear boy. Now
I'm being left behind . . . my old mind you see. I like old
fashioned things . . . Earl Gray tea, Sir Walter Scott,
Vaseline. Marmite is still delicious.

Phil   I've never tried Marmite.

Albert   . . . on toast . . . for breakfast . . . and kippers. I love a
good kipper. You must have breakfast with me sometime.

Phil   Oh . . .

Albert   . . . and if you can spare time from your studies,
perhaps you'll travel over to Glasgow with me for the opera.
Janet Baker's singing Dorabella in *Così fan tutte*. It should be
divine.

Phil   I'm busy at the moment . . . practical assessments this term and finals next. I've got a few holes in my course work file to be plugged. Maybe later in the summer, Albert.

Albert   I'll take you out for dinner . . . make a real evening of it. Well . . . I'll be going. When shall I see you?

Phil   I'm keeping myself to myself just now. I want to do well at college.

Albert   Very sensible. I haven't seen you at Scottish Minorities Group meetings recently.

Phil   No . . . it's all this reading I'm doing. I've no time.

Albert   Goodbye then. (*He leaves two five-pound notes by the bed.*)

Phil   See you, Albert.

Albert   No doubt . . . no doubt. (*He leaves.*)

Phil   My father drives long-distance lorries. I've got a whole brood of half-brothers and sisters scattered around the borders and beyond. I think my father carries the brotherhood of man too far. Some of it has rubbed off onto me. We meet . . . always by accident . . . sometimes when I'm out shopping there's this tremendous hooting and there's Father driving past waving at me . . . a big smile across his face. He rarely stops to talk. I suppose he treats all his progeny in the same manner. He's not on the phone and I can't keep track of the number of firms he works for. If I want to see him, I have to travel out to Wester Hailes on the off chance of him actually being there. He's a freelance like me.

Robert *bursts in.*

Robert   Phil . . . oh . . . Phil . . . I've been molested.

Phil   That's great news, Robert . . . I'm happy for you.

Robert   No . . . no . . .

Phil   Robert . . . I've got to eat shortly.

Robert   This man came in at lunch time . . . and he knew me.

Phil   What?

Robert He knows you too. He was a fascist . . . sent by the National Front . . . He wanted to suck me off . . .

Phil Maybe he was on a diet . . .

Robert He must have been one of yours . . . who was he?

Phil Sounds like Eddie . . . the lover of my mother's paramour . . .

Robert He frightens me.

Phil Don't worry . . . he's a psychopath.

Robert I don't want to be pursued by your insane relations.

Phil We don't know for certain it was Eddie. My family doesn't have a *monopoly* on Edinburgh's psychopaths . . . you did well this morning.

Robert Do you think so? I was absolutely quaking when I arrived. I was saying 'Robert . . . what have you let yourself in for . . . ' I was sure she was watching me extra carefully . . . so I got the jeans on the same coat hanger just like you said . . . then I was stuck with this spare hanger inside my jacket . . . I felt guilty . . . my knees were racing . . . absolutely quivering. So I was just off to the loo when she walks right over to me and says 'Where are you off to?' and I says 'The loo,' and she says 'You've only just come,' and I says 'So?' Are you listening?

Phil Nearly.

Robert And I says, 'I've been bursting all the way on the bus,' and she says, 'You just been, I was watching,' and I says, 'Oh no, I went to blow my nose on some bog roll,' and all the time I could feel it slipping down . . .

Phil What?

Robert The hanger . . . and it was three minutes to ten. It was like being in an Alistair McLean movie . . .

Phil Ahhh.

Robert . . . so I just pushed past her and went to the loo and whipped it out . . .

Phil What?

Robert   The screwdriver . . . and I took off the top of the cistern and shoved the hanger inside and screwed the top back on just like a bank robber.

Phil   Did you flush it?

Robert   Of course . . . So I was back in the shop just as you came in . . . it was good wasn't it? What are we doing tonight? Let's go out and celebrate.

Phil   I'm meeting up with Richard . . . this new guy at college. We're going to this German film . . . sub-titles . . .

Robert   Why didn't you ask me?

Phil   I'm asking you now. Come with us.

Robert   I don't want this other guy hanging around. I want to go out to the Dragon Pearl . . . just the two of us.

Phil   Do you fancy one of those denim waistcoats?

Robert   No!

Phil   Come with us. Make a threesome.

Robert   No!

Phil   I'm sorry, Robert. We'll go out tomorrow . . . go to the Loon Fung. Have you got any money?

Robert   I want to go out tonight . . . with you . . . alone.

Phil   I can't.

Robert   I go off people so quickly.

Phil   I'm just getting on with my life.

Robert   What about our life? I'm just company . . . someone to help pay the bills.

Phil   We're companions aren't we?

Robert   I've started cottaging again.

Phil   Friendships last longer than affairs . . . an affair . . . that's just playing games.

Robert   One of my punters took me to Nottingham a few months back.

Phil   Not *the* Nottingham?

Robert   Yes! We went to Shades . . . and the Pavilion . . .
had a great time together.

Phil   You can have a good weekend anywhere . . . it's the
weeks and weeks that are difficult. So what happened to your
Nottingham friend?

Robert   Didn't really fancy him. He had money . . . but I've
got my standards to look after . . . and you're still going with
Richard tonight?

Phil   Yes.

Richard *is out shopping. He has a bag of records that he's bought.*

Richard   Excellent . . . excellent! Pollini playing the
Chopin Études . . . only £1.90 from Boots . . . I'm sure they
got the prices mixed up . . . Solomon playing Mozart Piano
Concertos – a double album! . . . Wonderful perfomances . . .
only £2.50 . . . what an excellent outing. Edinburgh . . . I take
back all the rude things I've ever said about you! And Phil will
be waiting for me this evening . . . at least I think he will . . .
he will . . . of course he will. Now . . . I've just got time to get
back to my lodgings for my tea . . . and then I'm away out
again!

Phil *is walking past the Haymarket towards Princes Street. He meets*
Peter *the solicitor.*

Phil   Hi Peter . . .

Peter   Ah . . . now then . . . where are you off to you naughty
boy?

Phil   Oh . . . I'm meeting this guy later on . . . I thought I'd
call in at the Kenilworth for an hour or so.

Peter   Oh no you're not.

Phil   Why don't you come? You can buy the drinks.

Peter   I've got a better idea. Let's go back to the office. We
can raid the booze cupboard for nothing . . . and relax.

Phil   Oh . . . no . . . I'm not on tonight.

Peter   Have you heard about my recital? I'm giving a
recital next Thursday . . . to a selected audience at my flat . . .
Lieder . . . Schubert, Mahler . . . and Wolfe . . . £2 a ticket in
aid of SMG funds.

Phil   Have you sold any yet?

Peter   Of course. Not many . . . I have a following you
know . . . they'll flock on the night.

Phil   I've got to go.

Peter   Come back for a while. I've had a lousy day . . .
conveyancing, debt collecting . . . and this bloody idiot
complaining that leaves from his neighbour's tree are
blocking his gutters. I'll make it worth your while.

Phil   Do you promise not to invite me to your recital?

Peter   Right-oh . . . consider yourself under contract . . .

Phil   Just half an hour, mind . . . and no residual rights.

Robert *outside GHQ at the east end of Princes Street.*

Robert   Over there . . . the gents opposite the North British
Hotel . . . that's GHQ . . . the busiest cottage in Edinburgh.
I'll be down there in just a minute. There's always a chance of
scoring day or night . . . the chase quickens up around closing
time. I'm surprised Château Charles isn't here . . . he's an
institution . . . he's had more chickens than just about anyone
in town. He'd follow me down . . . not because he thinks
there's any chance with me . . . but just in case I've got
something in tow.

Robert *has gone down into GHQ and is pissing.*

We don't speak down here. The game's played silently most
of the time. We don't stay long either . . . the police keep an
eye open. Well . . . I've run dry . . . adjust my dress like a
gentleman. Nothing worth waiting for here. In and out's the
first rule of cottaging. Never hang around and you'll not get
caught. Mind . . . there is one guy who loves cottaging so
much that he spends his entire annual holidays at it each

year . . . travelling all over Scotland. He even takes a thermos and packed lunch with him . . . a sort of Egon Ronay.

I've had enough of trolling around . . . same bloody faces everywhere. I'm going to take a look in at the Traverse Theatre bar. Sometimes get trade in there . . .

Phil *meets* **Richard** *outside the film theatre.*

Phil   Sorry I'm late, Richard . . . I got held up . . .

Richard   Are you sure you want to go and see this?

Phil   Yes . . . look . . . you buy the tickets . . . there's the money.

He gives **Richard** *a five-pound note.*

Richard   I'll pay you in.

Phil   No . . . no . . . I just got the cash specially. I want you to buy the tickets though . . . like taking me to the pictures. Do this for me.

Richard   Right . . .

Phil   I want the change, mind . . .

They go into the cinema.

Robert *comes back to the apartment.*

Robert   This is the sort of evening that fills you with despair . . .

The Traverse bar was flat. I got talking a few times . . . just casual punters . . . but I couldn't get interested. About once every two months I get post-pubescent menopause . . . that's the way I feel tonight.

Generally I don't bother with those theatrical wankers anyway . . . they're all into themselves. They try and talk all posh and intellectual as though they are where it's at . . . but underneath you get the feeling their Y-fronts could do with a good wash . . . and they're always broke . . . except for buying themselves drinks . . .

I never drink . . . only fruit juices and coke. I'm in training,
you see. When I score I like to know what's happening . . . and
cope better than the other guy. I take a pride in myself. With
the right man I can come all night . . . thanks to Coca-Cola.

At last **Phil** *arrives back with* **Richard**.

Phil We've had a great time. This is Richard.

Richard Hello.

Phil This is Robert. We share this place.

Robert What was the animal film like?

Phil Don't take any notice. I'll make some coffee. You
want any coffee, Robert?

Robert Of course.

Phil Oh . . . Richard . . . do you like tartan shirts? Would
they go well with these jeans?

Robert Don't answer.

Phil Robert works in a men's shop . . . he gets things at cost
price. Would you like a lumber jack's shirt, Richard?

Richard I've never really thought about it.

Robert Do you fancy that? I don't . . . I've gone right off it.
I'm just his vassel.

Phil Why am I making you coffee then?

Richard Nice place you've got here.

Robert Your friend's got a sincerity problem, Philip . . .

Phil Two sugars, Richard?

Richard Yes, please.

Phil Would you like to see my photographs? I was staying
with this guy down in London. I answered this advertisement
in *Gay News*. He had me to stay for Christmas . . . took me all
over. Where's the viewer, Robert?

Robert Don't bother.

Richard Well I'd like to see them.

Robert The batteries are flat.

Phil How do you know?

Robert I took them out to use in the vibrator . . . they're finished . . .

Phil That's my vibrator you cunt . . . buy your own bloody equipment.

Robert It was that deputy headmaster you introduced me to . . . Richard . . . he wanted to put me into a strait-jacket next time round. Be grateful you didn't lose it. It scuttled up him like an Olympic mole . . . I thought it was going to be a hospital job at first. Are you staying here the night?

Richard No.

Robert Good! We share a room and I'm dying to get some sleep. Do you know what it's like to play twelfth man?

Phil You may wake up dead tomorrow.

Robert How are you settling in at college, Richard?

Phil Oh, Richard . . . I'm full of work just now . . . there's so much to do. I haven't had a man for weeks. I'm right off men, in fact . . . till I've got my essays done.

Robert Isn't it pathetic . . .

Phil Help me, Richard. I've got my assessment in two weeks. I'm in the opening five pages of *Waiting for Godot*. Help me with my Vladimir. Please, Richard.

Robert He pleads like a little child when he wants anything.

Richard You'll make a good tramp without my help.

Robert Haaaaaaaa . . .

Phil I'll bring them to college.

Richard What?

Phil The photographs. I'll get some new batteries . . . I'll show you at lunch time. I had a wild time down in London, Richard. I was in the Colherne one night . . . got picked up by this guy . . . all leather and chains with a chest like a door mat. I thought he'd be different. I went back to his place and he tried to murder me . . . he did . . . he picked up this carving

knife and started waving it around . . . then he pinned me to
the bed and said he was going to punish me for walking the
streets . . . then he wanted to piss on me and I got up and fled
out of the room and flew into the Boltons and told the lads
what had happened . . . and they laughed, Richard . . . Have
some more coffee? Would you like a biscuit?

Richard   I'm away home now.

Phil   Stay a bit longer . . . I'm not ready for bed yet.

Robert   I am.

Richard   So am I. Thanks for the coffee. Good night,
Robert. I'll see you again.

Robert   Really?

Phil   Oh . . . well . . . good night Richard . . . I'll see you
tomorrow.

Richard   Yes.

Richard *leaves.*

Robert   Good!

Phil   I hate you. When do I go on against your friends like
that?

Robert   I haven't got any friends.

Phil   You know what I mean. I like Richard. He won't
come back now.

Robert   Like a bet?

Phil   Why are you so aggressive?

Robert   I hate being surplus to your requirements . . .
discontinued stock.

Phil   You're not . . . What have you been doing tonight?
Why are you so bitter? I keep trying to please everyone. We're
sharing, aren't we?

Robert   I want more . . .

Phil   What more is there? You're going to walk out on me.
Like all the others. You've got a good base here. You've got a
job. A month ago you were lousy around the streets. What are

you going to do? Go back to the Spider. He'll welcome you
back.

Robert   I'm not going back to the Spider. No way. But I
wouldn't mind taking another trip down south of the border.

Phil   Don't leave me, Robert . . . not yet . . .

Robert   I'm not leaving right now.

Phil   I'll make you another coffee. Don't move . . . I'll do
it . . . I'll get you a nice present . . . would you like a lumber-
jack shirt? I'd like one . . . let's do it tomorrow . . . ten o'clock.

Robert   No . . .

Evening. **Eddie** *on the streets following* **Phil**.

Eddie   I was born on Tyneside . . . but I came to Leith with
my mother when I was a bairn so I want to believe I'm
Scottish through and through. Well I am! But I still go back to
Newcastle once a year to visit my granny. She's ninety-three
and lives off Westgate Hill behind these bike shops. There's a
whole road of them there, you know. And swap shops. They
have swap shops too . . . down there they do. Geordies can't
afford to buy things from new. Not all the time like we do.
They can't help it. I've got nothing against Geordies . . . I
mean . . . it's not their fault is it? I've had a Scottish education
and that gives you opportunities . . . you know . . . to think for
yourself. To tell the truth I hate fucking Geordies. Except for
my granny. She can't help it either.

Eddie *overhears the following scene with* **Spider**.

Phil *is walking past the National Gallery.* **Spider** *accosts him.*

Spider   Phil . . . where are you off to?

Phil   Hello Spider. How's things? I like your new wig.

Spider   You should have seen my curly perm. The lads kept
passing me the dirty saucepans for weeks . . . and how's young
Robert surviving with you?

Phil   Fine.

Spider   He was special vintage . . . to me he was . . . lucky bastard . . .

Phil   Special to me too.

Spider   . . . and he's got a job . . . an appropriate job, I gather. He still owes me for the shoes . . . £15. That's three nights he owes, Phil. There'll be interest to pay soon. Spider always gets his way in the end. You know that. Tell him I'm still waiting . . . and I have a lovely young thing staying at the minute . . . down from Aberdeen. You would enjoy him immensely. Brisk . . . elegant . . . with a heavenly bouquet. I have decanted him and am sipping slowly to the last drop. Why don't you come to supper one night? You can be the brandy. The boys would love to entertain you.

Phil   I'm busy with finals at the moment.

Spider   . . . and you're going to run off and leave me . . .

Phil   I'm meeting someone.

Eddie *doesn't know which one to follow. He follows* **Spider**.

Eddie   Poofs!

Richard *at the Dalry Road flat.* **Phil** *is in the bathroom.*

Richard   A few days after the film, we spent another evening together. We had a meal at some Chinese place . . . the Loon Fung? Something like that? Lemon chicken . . . excellent . . . and we went for a drink afterwards.

He talked . . . the way he does. Then, at closing time, I was just going to drive him back to his place, when he goes and picks up a complete stranger . . . in the Kenilworth this was . . . and expected me to drive them both back to the Dalry Road.

I did.

I just couldn't bring myself to tell him to fuck off home himself. So when the three of us got back to his apartment . . . well . . . he just left me standing there . . . said he was too tired to ask me in for coffee. It was just simple rejection of me for the evening. He'd finished with me, you see. I didn't want anything from him. It hurt me.

The next day he's all over me again at college . . . wanting me
to come round here for tea. First he's going to do his Vladimir
for me . . . then he says he'll leave it to the assessment . . .
then . . . when I come here . . . he's got his full Vladimir outfit
on . . . and I have to read Estragon . . . while he leaps around
the room trying to remember his lines. He's only doing the
first bit of the play . . . not the whole thing . . .

He's in the bathroom . . . changing . . .

Phil *comes out of the bathroom. He has been cleaning himself up. He is
still wearing his Vladimir trousers, but is undressed above the waist. He
is drying himself with a towel.*

Phil   What did you think?

Richard   Do you really want to know?

Phil   Of course. I don't have to believe you.

Richard   No, you don't.

Phil   So?

Richard   Sit down. There are three things that I can help
you with. But you are going to have to start your production
all over again.

Phil   There's the other boy as well.

Richard   OK . . . well listen and see what you think. First of
all, you've got a problem with this Faber text of the play. It's
full of the most precise stage directions – telling you all the
business . . . where to pause . . . what tone of voice to use. What
that really amounts to is a record of a previous production.
What you should do first is type out the script and leave out all
the stage directions. Go through that script with your friend
and try and discover its sense. If you are totally stuck, refer
back to the Faber edition to see if it helps in any way . . .

Phil   Could you type it out for us?

Richard   I could . . . but I'm not going to. You must do it.
You'll learn something about the bones of the play.

Phil   OK.

Richard Secondly . . . you may decide that your tramp costume is what you want. But take a look at some paintings. Picasso, perhaps? People forced out on the road. Desperate. Isolated. We'll check out the library together. Tomorrow lunchtime? And thirdly . . . do you want any more?

Phil Yes.

Richard This is more personal to you. There's very little music in your voice. You don't phrase things imaginatively. You time the faster exchanges well . . . and sharply . . . but whenever you get a longer bit, you never give it time to breathe . . . to live . . . I don't get any feeling of a real person behind the words. Now . . . hold on . . . I'm going to buy you a record! It's of Puccini arias sung by Maria Callas. She plays a whole lot of different characters and characterises them wonderfully . . . it's the slight changes in tone of the voice . . . the way she phrases things . . . the way she is able to give meaning to the simplest . . . or what seem to be the simplest phrases of music. You can hear what interpretation really means. It's wonderful, Phil. To play Vladimir well, you've got to try to bring to the part the same intense illumination . . . to every bit of it . . .

Phil I'm going to get changed.

Richard OK.

Phil *doesn't want to say anything. He finds his clothes, which are scattered around the place and gets dressed.*

Phil Are you bored with me yet?

Richard No.

Phil You're angry though?

Richard I was.

Phil About last night?

Richard Yes.

Phil Why?

Richard You know why.

Phil I want to hear you tell me.

Richard Just picking someone up. Leaving me on the doorstep.

Phil You could do that too. I'll get you anyone you want, Richard. Just tell me *what* you want . . .

He needed a bed for the night . . .

Richard You gave him more than a bed.

Phil So?

Richard It's rejection, Phil . . .

Phil I don't want to hurt you, Richard. Just don't be like all the others . . .

Richard Why do you hate kissing?

Phil Me?

Richard Yes.

Phil I . . . well . . . I don't hate it. There's only a few people I kiss on the mouth . . . my mother. I don't like it, that's all.

Richard You'll suck someone off, but you won't kiss them. Is that it?

Phil Do you think I'm trash?

Richard Sometimes. Not really.

Phil Richard, I don't fancy you sexually.

Richard What's that got to do with it?

Phil I would sleep with you. If you wanted.

Richard I don't.

Phil I won't hurt you again. Don't look at me like that! You don't turn me on, Richard.

Richard So what?

Phil You're honest. I think you are. That's rare. It's worth something. It's not your body. There's nothing wrong with your body. I could get off on it. Look! You're not just another fucking punter! You despise me. You think I'm trash.

Richard No.

Phil I am. I am. Last week this guy from London was staying at the North British. I promised to find him a boy. Me playing the pimp. I went round all the bars. No one young enough for Douglas was on. I kept phoning him at the hotel, telling him not to worry . . . not to go out . . . be patient. Then I tracked down Pip. He's just fourteen and I said please do this for me and he made me promise that I wouldn't leave him alone with Douglas so I promised and when Douglas saw Pip he was so excited! So pleased! I love pleasing people.

And he gave us both a drink and there we were drinking whisky and this man touching up Pip . . . unzipping him and me just looking on. And Pip . . . he's massive for a fourteen-year-old . . . and Douglas slides down Pip's jeans and he's amazed at what he sees, Richard. And he gets the bottle of whisky and starts pouring it over Pip's cock and Pip says it stings and we start to laugh and there's this guy lapping it up off Pip's cock and Pip and I are in hysterics. And I was feeling left out of things so I put my arms around Pip and started to pull myself off. And Douglas . . . he finished me off . . . and then Pip came in his mouth. And Douglas was so pleased! He really liked it, Richard. And he said he'd spend another night in Edinburgh. Edinburgh was a great city. And he wanted me to find him another boy for the next day. And he gave me £20 and Pip £10.

I really am trash, Richard.

Richard Did you find him another boy?

Phil He left town, that night. On the sleeper. He'll be back. They all come back, Richard. So will you.

Richard Are you sure?

Phil I'm interested in what you said about Vladimir. Starting again is hard, Richard. I have a date with Estragon tomorrow. We'll look at your pictures. You stay out of it. I'll tell him what you said.

Richard *starts to go*.

Richard 'You're angry?'

Phil 'Forgive me.'

Richard 'Come, give me your hand.'

Phil 'Embrace me! Don't be stubborn!'

Richard (*rejecting him*) 'You stink of . . .'

Phil I hate garlic.

Richard Sweat . . . whisky . . .

Phil I . . . quite like whisky . . .

Richard *leaves*.

Phil *studies* Waiting for Godot.

Maria Callas sings the 'Principessa Lo-u-Ling . . .' section from 'In questa reggia' from Turandot.

Eddie *is walking the streets after closing time with a can of beer and a carry-out. He tries to cross the road and is nearly run over.*

Eddie Poof!

He presses the button on the pelican crossing.

You know . . . if I hadn't been a thinker I'd like to have been an artist. At least I think I would. Hitler had the same problem. I'm going to write a book . . . one of these days I will. *The Vengeance of the Lone Wolf.* You see when I was a kid I always wanted to be a redskin. That was before I realised they were sub-human, of course. I know that now. That's what stops me writing it . . .

The pelican crossing starts bleeping and **Eddie** *crosses the road.*

At the Dalry Road flat, **Phil** *is having a bath.* **Robert** *is trying to tidy up.*

Robert That deputy head . . . I only went with him for money. He gave me more than I would have asked for. He understands. He'll come back for more. No strait-jackets though. You never know what'll happen with a new guy. It's just as well to have someone like Phil around. He knows the game backwards. He's been playing it a year or two longer than I have. I'm eighteen. I'm no chicken.

Phil (*off*)   Robert . . . Robert . . .

Robert   Doesn't it make you sick. He even needs me when he's having a bath.

Phil (*off*)   Robert . . .

Robert   What?

Phil (*off*)   Could you bring in the shampoo?

Robert   Where is it?

Phil (*off*)   On the table.

Robert *finds it and takes it into the bathroom. He returns.*

Phil (*off*)   Robert . . .

Robert   What?

Phil (*off*)   Come back . . .

Robert   I'm busy.

Phil (*off*)   Please . . .

Robert   Ohhhhh . . .

Robert *goes through to him.*

Phil (*off*)   Scrub my back.

Robert (*off*)   Poor little boy . . . you haven't got your ducks. Would you like your ducks?

Phil (*off*)   Thanks . . . I said thanks . . . ahhhhhh . . .

Robert *re-enters.*

Robert   My first visit to Edinburgh . . . didn't know where to go. Didn't need to as it turned out. Château Charles spotted me half way down Princess Street . . . fox among the chickens. He had me the once . . . that first visit. It was what I came for, mind. There's money to be made. Wouldn't you pull a guy off for £30. Well . . . £5? I've made £30 during the Festival. The price of everything goes up then. I mean . . . the Festival's bloody rent, isn't it? You've got to get your sense of values right. If an opera ticket's worth £15, a night with a highly skilled rent-boy's worth at least £50 . . .

Phil *enters in his towel.*

Phil Robert . . . you've tidied up.

Robert I've just re-arranged the mess.

Phil I'm happy.

Robert Does that mean you're going to keep me awake all night?

Phil Don't be angry with me.

Robert Leave me alone.

Phil Why do you go on rejecting me?

Robert Me?

Phil I'll make you a coffee.

Robert I don't want any.

Phil What would you like?

Robert Nothing. Let's go to bed.

Phil OK. We'll go to bed. Would you like me to read you a bedtime story?

Robert No.

Phil I'll tell you one, then.

There are two single beds. **Robert** *undresses.*

Robert I don't want one.

Phil Thanks for the denim waistcoat.

Robert Stop crawling. I don't want to talk to you.

Phil 'No one ever suffers but you . . . I don't count.'

Robert I've still got those spots.

Phil Let's see . . . ummm . . . heat rash.

Robert They don't itch or anything.

Phil Do they come out to feed?

Robert No.

Phil I'll give you a splash just in case.

His bedside locker is full of medications. **Phil** *gets out the bottle of benzyl benzoate.*

I'll do it. Shake the bottle. There . . .

He rubs some into **Robert***'s stomach.*

Now get into bed like a good boy. Oh no . . . my pills . . . a curse on NSU . . .

Phil *gets out his bottle of pills and goes to the bathroom.*

Robert   There's rabies on the continent and it's moving northwards.

Phil *returns with a glass of water and swallows his pills.*

Phil   I'd rather foam at the mouth than pee glass. I get every bloody thing. Wait till you've had a dose front and back.

Robert   No thanks.

Phil   Have you been helping yourself to my Esoderm?

Robert   Oh . . . it was that guy I met at the SMG meeting.

Phil   I wish you'd get your own medications . . . and your own batteries. North Sea oil's not going to bring down the price of crab lotion.

Robert   I thought Boots gave you a free bottle with every tube of KY you buy there.

Phil   Who was he anyway?

Robert   Who?

Phil   At SMG.

Robert   Holyrood Harry!

Phil   Ohhhh . . . I don't believe it.

Robert   He's been chasing for months.

Phil   What did he do for you?

Robert   He's got this massive double-double bed, and I was doused with your Esoderm after a night with Fire Officer Jimmy. I told Harry I didn't want anything. He said he just wanted company for the night. He brought me coffee in bed. That was nice. I like being looked after.

Phil   I look after you. I'm a one-man canteen.

Robert   So I left my Marks and Spencers knics on and told him to leave it that way. Then he started playing up and before I knew what was happening he was upside down and . . .

Phil   Foul, foul . . . oh foul . . .

Robert   He loved it.

Phil   Spare me.

Robert   . . . and he came all over my face.

Phil   Ohhhhhhh . . .

Robert   . . . and he screamed as he came . . .

Phil   No . . .

Robert   . . . like this . . . Aaaaahhhhhhhhhhhh . . . ahhh . . .

Phil   And was Holyrood struck by vengeful thunderbolts?

Robert   . . . and he gave me £10.

Phil   What? Harry did?

Robert   He wants me back again.

Phil   It stinks. Stinks. The whole world is rotten and I'm rotting away with it. My bowels are full of itching powder. We're all on hooks . . . like bait on hooks . . . and we wriggle around while there's life in us and the hook tears . . . and the punters gather round . . . and we're eaten and eaten . . . and the rent we get goes on rent-food, rent-electricity, rent-bloody-everything. I'm dying, Robert. And I love it.

Robert   You're not dying . . . you're just a Scottish drama student.

Phil   . . . and I've got to be Vladimir in a week's time. 'There's a man all over for you, blaming his boots for the faults of his feet . . .'

Robert   I'm tired. Let's go to sleep now.

Phil   I'll turn out the light.

Robert   Good night.

Phil   Good night.

Robert   It's been a good day.

Phil   Do we have any choice?

Robert   What?

Phil   Is there any alternative to bloody rent?

The door bell rings.

Oh shit.

Robert   Oh bugger.

Phil   Yours.

Robert   No . . . yours.

Phil   That's half the Edinburgh Fire Brigade.

Robert   That's half the Scottish Opera chorus.

Phil *answers the door. It's* **Richard**. *He's been drinking. He conceals a bunch of wilted flowers.*

Richard   Sorry . . . sorry . . . I'm very sorry. These are for you.

He gives **Phil** *the flowers.*

Phil   Oh God. Come in.

Richard   I've been out. Oh . . . you're already . . . oh . . . is there someone here? Oops . . . do you mind if I sit down?

Phil   You shouldn't have come, Richard. We've gone to bed.

Richard   Have you? Who? Oh.

Phil   Just Robert and me. Robert's tired. So am I. Why don't you go home, Richard.

Richard   Home? Oh yes . . . I don't want to. I'm being honest with you. You don't mind me being honest? I'm sorry . . . I'm . . . I've been out.

Robert *(from the bedroom)*   Who is it?

Phil   See . . . you've woken up my friend.

Richard   I'm not a stranger. Why are you talking to me as though I'm a stranger?

Phil *goes through to* **Robert**.

Phil It's bloody Richard. He's pissed. These are for me.

Robert Oh . . . has he brought me any?

Phil I thought I'd let him bring you the deadly nightshade himself.

Robert Send him home . . . please . . .

Phil I have a horrible feeling he wants to stay the night.

Robert No . . . and that's my last word on the matter.

Phil *goes back to* **Richard**.

Phil Robert says 'hi'. Where did you get these things?

Richard They were discarded on the street. I brought them straight to you. I also have this . . . (*He produces half a bottle of whisky.*) . . . which I thought might help to pass an hour or so of this bloody night.

Phil Wait there.

Phil *goes back to* **Robert**.

He has presented us with half a bottle of whisky.

Robert That must be the meanest act. We're not worth a whole bottle. What further proof do you want? Send him away.

Phil Are you inciting me to cruelty?

Richard (*outside*) Can I come in?

Robert No!

Richard Sorry.

Phil *goes back to* **Richard**.

Richard All right . . . I'll go . . . you don't have to say it. I'll go . . .

Phil Robert's had enough, Richard. I don't want to cast you out into the streets. Have you got a car here?

Richard Yes . . . yes . . . it's outside . . . that's . . . well . . . that's what I was thinking.

Phil   I wasn't thinking anything. I just wanted to make sure you got home safely.

Richard   Look . . . would you . . . perhaps it's unfair to ask . . .

Robert *comes through from the bedroom.*

Richard   . . . but . . . come back tonight . . . to my place.

Robert   No, he won't. He's staying here with me.

Phil   Robert, you're interfering.

Richard   No . . . no . . . Robert's right. I shouldn't have asked. I shouldn't have come here tonight . . . I'm . . . well . . . I was lonely . . . that's all.

Robert   . . . and pissed.

Phil (*to* **Robert**)   Why are you so fucking unpleasant?

Robert   How else am I supposed to protect myself from you?

Richard   I'll go now. Good night gentlemen.

Phil   Wait . . . I'll get dressed.

Richard   No. You're staying here. I'm absolutely in the wrong in this. Robert . . . I didn't mean . . . I had no idea . . . I can't say it properly . . . but good night . . .

Richard *leaves.* **Phil** *and* **Robert** *get back into their own beds.*

Robert   Come in with me.

Phil   No.

Robert   I'm sorry about Richard . . . all your other punters are just punters. If he ever comes back I'll treat him better . . .

Phil   What are you like?

Robert   Please Phil.

Phil   Bloody hell!

Phil *gets in with* **Robert**.

Phil   Shove over!

He turns out the light.

Robert   Oh God . . . I'm selling bloody jeans at nine o'clock tomorrow . . .

Phil   Are you saying your prayers?

Robert   What are you doing?

Phil   I'm dancing at eleven . . .

Robert   Serves you right you stupid poof.

Phil   Don't walk out on me, Robert. I need you with me.

Robert   I won't. Not yet.

Act Two

Robert *is back at the flat on a Wednesday afternoon.* **Richard** *is having a bath next door.*

Robert I only get one afternoon a week off and I like my Wednesdays to myself. Phil doesn't usually get in till 5.30 or 6. I've got the whole place to myself. That's good. I'm not used to having my own territory. Then Richard turns up. There's no hot water at his place in the afternoon so he's come round here for a bath . . .

Richard (*off*) Robert . . .

Robert He's caught this off Phil . . . or is it something in me? Would I make my fortune as a baths attendant?

Richard (*off*) Please Robert . . .

Robert Another pleader . . . what?

Richard (*off*) Can I use some shampoo?

Robert Did he have to ask that? *Yes . . .*

Richard (*off*) Thank you.

Robert Phil's been at his little games again. This time it's advertising in *Gay News*. 'Scottish intellectual youth with interest in urban blood sports seeks wealthy Highland gentlemen.' That's gentle*men*, please note. He's had half a dozen replies . . . most of them from south of the border . . . one from Arizona. Two replies came separately from two men living at the same address in Auchtertool. He's arranged a rendezvous with both of them at the same time and the same place, asking each to wear a red rose in his buttonhole.

Richard *enters in a towel.*

Robert You're smothered in my Denim talc.

Richard . . . for the man who doesn't have to try too hard.

Robert I wish you'd get dressed. Your flesh threatens me.

Richard Oh. Sorry.

Richard *goes back to the bathroom.*

Robert And that's Richard in a nutshell. Did it occur to him that I might like being threatened? I'm assuming that his unannounced arrival this afternoon was planned. He knew somehow that I'd be here and alone. But he's a born failure . . . and hard to get excited about. I mean . . . most men clean and hot from a bath . . . sprinkled liberally with Denim and swathed in an easily penetrated towel would arouse at the very least my curiosity. But Richard actually makes me angry. He won't speak out on his own behalf . . . from his heart. I mean . . . what goes on inside that man? What is he really after? I'm not coping with him at all. He's confusing me. Oh Richard, leave us in peace. Go back to Tyneside.

Richard *returns clothed.*

Richard Is that better?

Robert Not really. Let's say things we can understand. What do you want of me? Why are you here?

Richard I came to have a bath.

Robert (*aside*) I can't talk to this man. (*To* **Richard**.) Why not read *Gay News*? There are record reviews . . . bits about the theatre and other escapist twaddle.

Richard How much do you make on the streets each week?

Robert Don't talk to me like that.

Richard You wanted me to talk about things we can understand.

Robert You don't know anything about it.

Richard I sell myself as a lecturer.

Robert So?

Richard I'd like you to come out with me tonight.

Robert What?

Richard   We can have something to eat . . . go and see a film . . . anything you want.

Robert   I don't know what's on.

Richard   Does it matter?

Robert   It does if we're going out to the cinema. I don't know whether I want to go out. I don't know what I want to do. I haven't got any money.

Richard   I'll pay you in.

Robert   I don't know what Phil's doing.

Richard   . . . rehearsing his assessment . . .

Robert   I don't know.

Richard   I'll be in the K at 6.30 . . . if you want to join me.

Robert   I'll think about it. I'm not promising.

Richard   I'm not promising either. We'll leave it like this. *If* I'm at the K at 6.30 and you happen to come in and find me there . . . and *if* we want to spend the rest of the evening together . . . and *if* I've got enough money in my pocket . . . we *might* go and see a film.

Robert   . . . and have something to eat?

Richard   We'll leave it vague.

Robert   Yes.

Richard   I'm going now. Thanks for the bath.

Robert   Richard . . .

Richard   Yes?

Robert   Take care.

Richard   Yes.

Richard *leaves*.

Phil *is outside his mother's apartment. He is carrying a bag full of dirty washing.*

Phil   My mother lives here in Leith with this other woman . . . She's AC/DC actually. The pair of them are famous local personalities . . . they're known all over as 'Mop and Bucket'. It's true! Kids stop them in the streets down by the docks and ask, 'Which are you? Mop or Bucket?'

Home life was always a bit chaotic . . . it was great fun . . . this was when I was a kid myself . . . I wouldn't have missed a minute of it. My mother's Mop, by the way. When I tell stories about them nobody believes me . . . but they're all absolutely true. They fight all the time . . . moaning on at each other and busting the place up regularly. But they're inseparable. A few years back I was meeting this boy in Kenilworth . . . he was an art student at the university or something like that. Anyway, Mother was still living with Father at that time and I crashed right into Mother and Norma, alias 'Bucket' . . . me and this other boy . . . I thought he was great because he has this white fleck in his hair and I thought how marvellous it was to have a white fleck in your hair and be so young and we always made love with the light on or in daylight so I could watch his hair bobbing up and down . . . we screwed all over the city . . . up Carlton Hill . . . in the rockery of the Botanical Gardens . . . on the top of a 37 bus . . . I was so innocent in those days. Anyway . . . back in the Kenilworth . . . Mother stared at me and I stared back and saw who she was with and it suddenly dawned on me what was going on and I started to laugh and I went over and the four of us had a great time that evening . . . like getting to know your own mother all over again for the first time. She's great! She does my dirty washing once a fortnight and gives me tea.

Robert *is back at the flat with a punter,* **Thomas** *from Harpenden, a teacher.*

Thomas It's a better paid post you see, I'm only on scale 2 in Harpenden. Did you go to school in Edinburgh?

Robert No.

Thomas Where then? Where did you go? Oh . . . you don't have to tell me, I suppose. Do you think I'm doing the right thing?

Robert   I don't know.

Thomas   I like Edinburgh, you see. When I was training
we used to come up here during the Festival. I helped on one
of the fringe shows once. The students did this play . . . forget
what it was now. Oh . . . *This Way to the Tomb* . . . someone
called Duncan. I was the critic. I had to sit in the audience
and shout out something at the right time. It was dreadful if
the actors got in a muddle. I didn't know where I was
supposed to come in. The audience was supposed to think this
was an unsolicited interruption. Trouble was . . . I was the
audience some nights . . . just about, at least. It was terribly
long. There were monks in it. This was before Ken Russell.
God knows who chose it. Am I cheering you up?

Robert   No.

Thomas   It doesn't matter.

Robert   Ohhh . . .

Thomas   No really. You seem to be taking it very badly. I
can't get it up sometimes . . . happens to everybody.

Robert   You're old. I'm only eighteen. I'm supposed to be
in my prime.

Thomas   Oh . . . this is your prime is it? I'm postponing
mine as long as possible. Look. Don't be an idiot. It doesn't
matter anyway.

Robert   Don't go on about it.

Thomas   Then I got involved in this dance drama. That's
what it was called in those days. I had to do this dance with
this girl. Something about a night club . . . and taking her
back to my place . . . a failed seduction. The audience howled
as soon as I came on stage. The place was packed. I thought,
God they're going to love this. We thought it was serious in
rehearsals. They just fell about. The girl . . . she nearly
collapsed with embarrassment . . . an ordeal by ridicule. We
went through with it. By the end the audience was shouting
and hooting. I mean . . . Fonteyn and Nureyev were a disaster
compared with us. The students showered us with ferns and
geraniums . . . the fresh soil still clinging. I was bought free

drinks for weeks after. Poor girl had a nervous breakdown. Am I boring you?

Robert   Tremendously.

Thomas   Do you want me to go?

Robert   Yes please.

Thomas   But I don't want to leave you like this. There's no need to be unhappy. I mean . . . over what happened. We're not trying to prove anything, are we? I mean . . . I just came back with you for fun. And I've really enjoyed myself here. Well . . . if I get the job, can I make contact with you again? I may not get it of course. What the hell anyway. But I'd like to know someone.

Robert   I may not be here then.

Thomas   You moving?

Robert   I haven't decided.

Thomas *leaves a five-pound note.*

Thomas   Well . . . maybe I'll see you?

Robert   Maybe.

Phil *enters.*

Thomas   Oh . . . I'm just going.

Thomas *leaves.*

Phil   Who's that?

Robert   I can't remember.

Phil   Are you glad to see me back?

Robert   Should we celebrate?

Phil   . . . he didn't beat you?

Robert   Beat me?

Phil   . . . but for me where would you be? You'd be nothing more than a little heap of bones at the present minute, no doubt about it.

Robert   Stop your blathering.

Phil   Will you help me . . . please.

Robert   I'm not in the mood.

Phil   Please . . . I'm practising my assessment. I need support, Robert. Do you know what this is? I only want you to read Estragon. Here . . . right at the beginning. It's not asking much.

Robert   I hate bloody plays.

Phil   You've only got to read it. I've got to learn the bugger.

Robert   Pip came round.

Phil   What? Why didn't you tell me?

Robert   I haven't had a bloody chance, have I!

Phil   What did he want?

Robert   . . . said he wants to speak to you . . . I don't know.

Phil   I don't want him round here. Christ . . . why can't people just stay out of my life? Everything piles on top of you. Damn this play. Get on with it.

Robert   You start . . . 'So there you are again . . .'

Phil (*memory*)   'So there you are again . . .'

Robert (*reading*)   'Am I?'

Phil   'I'm glad to see you back. I thought you were gone for ever.'

Robert   'Me too.'

Phil   'Together again at last! Get up till I embrace you.'

Robert   No.

Phil   'We'll have to celebrate this. But how? Get up till I embrace you.'

Robert   'Not now. Not now.'

Phil   'May one enquire where His Highness spent the night?'

Robert   This is a pantomine . . . *Poof in Boots* . . .

Phil   *Dick and the Beanstalk.*

Robert   *Hello Sinbad.*

Phil   Get on with it.

Robert   'In a ditch.'

Phil   'A ditch! Where?'

Robert   'Over there.'

Phil   'And they didn't beat you?'

Robert   'Beat me? Certainly they beat me . . .' Is this an S & M production?

Phil   'The same lot as usual?'

Robert   'The same? I don't know.'

Phil   'When I think of it . . . all these years . . . but for me where would you be? You'd be nothing more than a little heap of bones at the present minute, no doubt about it.' Did Pip leave a message? Did he look worried?

Robert   ' . . . and what of it?'

Phil   What did he say?

Robert   Nothing. I told you. Hurry up.

Phil   'It's too much for one man. On the other hand what's the good of losing heart now, that's what I say. We should have thought of it a million years ago, in the nineties.'

Robert   'Ah stop blathering and help me off with this bloody thing.' It's daft this.

Phil   'Hand in hand from the top of the Eiffel Tower, among the first. We were presentable in those days. Now it's too late. They wouldn't even let us up.' What are you doing?

Robert   I'm fed up.

Phil   Why don't you help me? Just a little. I need help . . . Robert?

Robert   I'm away out with Richard tonight.

Phil   Richard?

Robert   Yes. He came round for a bath.

Phil   What? What happens in this place when I'm away? I can't cope. I thought you hated him.

Robert   Oh . . . no . . . not really. I'm getting used to him now. I pretend not to like him . . . oh . . . it's not that either . . . but he's offered to take me out . . . that's kind . . . after what happened last week.

Phil   Maybe he enjoys punishment. What are you going to do?

Robert   See a film. Go for a drink. I don't know. Talk?

Phil   He'll whisk you out of the K into the coffee bar next door.

Robert   That's OK by me. What does it matter to you anyway? He's joined your growing pile of rejects.

Phil   'No one ever suffers but you. I don't count. I'd like to hear what you'd say if you had what I have.'

Robert   Oh God . . . not another dose.

Phil   You're so close to me. I mean physically close. But you're nowhere. You hardly exist. It wouldn't matter if you came or went or vanished into thin air . . . because you don't realise or do anything to *help me, Robert*!

Robert   You're bloody mental . . .

Phil   ' . . . funny . . . '

Robert   Why don't you help me?

Robert *leaves*.

Phil   ' . . . nothing to be done . . . '

Richard *is in the café next to the Kenilworth.* **Robert** *is fetching two cups of coffee.* **Richard** *has been buying more records.*

Richard   This really is special! Furtwängler conducting Bruckner's Ninth Symphony in Berlin in 1944. I've heard this performance on the radio, but have never been able to get a copy of it. It's a live performance, and the orchestra and the audience must have felt that the end of the world was at hand. The result is so astounding that you should only experience a record like this two or three times in a lifetime. I found this copy in a dingy, anonymous shop, hidden in an arcade. It cost me one pound.

We hear the opening moments of the performance . . . **Robert** *brings over two coffees.*

Richard We didn't like the atmosphere next door in the K, so we've come in here.

Robert I did London when I was sixteen. I was sick at first. Nowhere to go. So I headed for Piccadilly Circus . . . looking for punters. Well . . . somewhere to stay the night actually. So I stood outside this cinema with this lesbian film on. Whenever anyone got close I panicked. That was odd. I'd been on the game in Edinburgh, but London was different. I didn't know the territory, you see. Or the people. They're all bloody foreigners down there. Then I met this Chinese kid. He'd come from North Shields . . . all the way to bloody London. He'd got settled in. He took me to this boys' hostel . . . behind Leicester Square. The warden had made him a housemaster . . . or something. He was absolutely hairless . . . with golden skin . . . and butch as hell. I never looked back after that . . . had a great summer.

Richard I haven't got that sort of . . . energy. Back in Newcastle I go to an occasional CHE meeting. Sometimes I take a look in the Senate Bar. I never go to the Eldon . . . gets rough in there . . . sometimes at least. I'd rather keep myself to myself.

Robert I'm bored with Edinburgh. I want to make a break, Richard. I don't feel at home with Phil.

Richard You don't have to stay there.

Robert When I was a kid I used to love pirate books. I've always wanted to be captured by pirates . . . you know . . . nice pirates . . .

Richard Would I make a nice pirate?

Robert You're not part of a crew, Richard . . . you're more like marooned . . .

Richard Why don't you rescue me?

Robert Can you lend me some money?

Richard What for?

Robert I owe someone some money, Richard. I'm in trouble. I've got to pay it back.

Richard How much do you need?

Robert £25.

Richard What?

Robert I know it's a lot. What am I going to do, Richard?

Richard Tell me about it.

Robert Oh . . . it's this man . . . that's all . . . he lent me some money and he wants it back. I'm not safe around the streets till I've paid it. He's threatening me. I've got to pay him. I can do it tonight . . . I'll pay you back.

Richard When?

Robert At the weekend . . . when I get paid. You'll get it back, Richard.

Richard *gives him the money.*

Richard That's just about cleaned me out.

Robert Are you hungry? I'm starving. Let's go to the Dragon Pearl. I'll pay . . . you can be my guest for the evening . . .

Richard Don't worry. I'll use my Access card.

Robert You're a friend to me. I'm glad I found you. I need you, Richard.

Richard Need me?

Carlton Hill. **Eddie** *is following* **Robert** *and overhears the following encounter.*

Spider *tracks down* **Robert** *by night.*

Spider Butterfly boy . . . a night flight to Carlton Hill . . .

Robert Hello Spider.

Spider What treats have you for me tonight?

Robert   None at all.

Spider   Come . . . let me look at you. Dear me. Bags under your eyes. You need old Spider to take care of you again. Your bright colours are starting to fade a little. Has the sweet butterfly become a night moth? Don't turn away like that. You used to come to Spider for comfort . . . and protection.

Robert   I've got to go.

Spider   And what have you done with those expensive shoes I paid for? Where's the money? You owe me money. £15. You know how to pay. We can settle the matter so amicably.

Robert   Leave me alone.

Spider   I'll burn your pretty wings. I want something now.

Robert   I haven't got any money. I'm broke. I'll pay you later.

Spider   You don't need cash to pay your debts. Don't let's waste time. The boys will be pleased to see you.

Robert *gives him* £5.

Robert   That's all I've got. I'll pay the rest later.

Spider   Empty your pockets. I'll get what's due one way or another, you little bastard.

Robert   Fuck off.

Spider   Ah . . . more money . . .

Robert   Give me that.

Spider *knocks him to the ground.*

Spider   That's another £10 I've taken. You've been doing good trade lately.

He throws the rest of the money back at **Robert**.

That's yours. Why not start a fresh account sometime?

Spider *leaves* **Robert** *groping around in the dark for the rest of his money.*

Eddie *confronts* **Spider**.

Eddie   *Cunt!* Robert . . . fuck off out of here . . .

Robert *gathers the rest of his money and runs off.*

Eddie   Fucking queer cunt picking on wee laddies . . .

Spider   Let me go.

Eddie (*taking the money*)   I'll have this . . . and this . . . and this . . .

Spider   Be careful.

Eddie   Spider . . . aye . . . I know who you are . . . been following you, haven't I. Taking money off wens. You leave Robert alone . . . never go near him again.

Spider   Ahhhhhh . . . Robert is it? Such a sweet boy . . .

Eddie   Don't speak like that. Vermin . . .

Eddie *is preparing to belt* **Spider** *but* **Spider** *has got out a flick knife. He swings at* **Eddie** *and misses.*

Eddie   Ahhhh . . . knives is it? Come on pretty boy . . .

Spider *slashes again but* **Eddie** *catches his arm. He is about to grab the knife when* **Spider** *stabs him in the hand, leaving the knife sticking there with blood pouring from the wound.*

Eddie   Blood . . .

Spider *flees.*

Applause as **Phil** *takes a bow as Vladimir at his college assessment.*

Robert *is alone at the flat. He has been sitting in the dark, as though hiding. The doorbell rings. It's* **Richard**.

Richard   Are you alone?

Robert   Yes. Come on in.

Richard   I come hot foot from Phil's assessment.

Robert   Where is he?

Richard   Catching the bus. He wanted to see his mother.

Robert   Was she there?

Richard That's one way of putting it.

Robert What was it like?

Richard Odd. Competent. He has a good sense of timing. He reacted cleverly to the audience. He was performing to us, not concentrating on interpretation at all. It was certainly striking.

Robert Has he passed?

Richard I imagine so. Nothing to do with me. No one's interested in my opinion.

Robert I am.

Richard How kind.

Robert *is very affectionate.*

Robert Would you like a coffee?

Richard I feel really dark this evening. Don't move, Robert. I want your shadow near mine. There. I'm tired of college . . . and this city . . . and of bars . . . and wet streets. I really want to forget it all, Robert. I wish I was back in Newcastle tonight. I miss my own place.

Robert So do I.

Richard Aren't you happy here?

Robert Not really.

Richard How are you going to escape?

Robert I don't know.

Richard We're doing this Pirandello play at college . . . *Henry IV* . . . and it's difficult working out what's real . . . or perhaps . . . what's really happening . . . and what isn't. I feel like that right now. I don't know *how* you exist in my life . . . or what I'm doing here. What is holding us together, Robert? Or am I just making that up? Sometimes I think we're adopting each other like lost people. Perhaps we're brothers. You're my son. That's more realistic. Do you think you're my son?

Robert I don't know.

Richard If you're not, what on earth am I doing here?
Why do we meet? We're not lovers. Sometimes we're not even
friends. I need to understand things better, Robert.
Otherwise . . . I can't go any further. I shall just become too
aware of the hunger in your eyes . . . your unpaid bills. Why
don't I give you money, like a beggar in the street, and just
clear off out of your life?

Phil *enters still dressed as Vladimir. This time his Vladimir costume
shows the influence of* **Richard** *on his production. The costume and
make-up are blue, beggarly and sad . . . as in a Picasso.*

Phil Oh Robert . . .

Robert What a state.

Phil I'm a spent *force*. A shell. A husk. I have crossed and
crossed the Rubicon. Behind me lies debris. A scorched land.
And ahead . . . rejection and despair.

Richard You did quite well.

Phil I know thee not old man. What does it matter? It's all
games. Quite valueless. Unless you've paid your subscription
in full and pretend it has meaning.

Oh Richard . . . I've made a decision.

Richard Oh . . .

Phil . . . about when I leave college . . . I'm going into
business.

Richard Oh . . .

Phil I'm going to make as much money as I can . . .

Robert What sort of business?

Phil . . . so I can have a place of my own . . . my own
tenement off George Street. I'm going to keep the phones
ringing all over the city. I'll clean out all the cottages . . . the
clubs . . . the saunas . . . I'll haunt every hotel lobby . . . every
promising bar . . . until I've given my special list a complete
overhaul. I'll start an account with a building society! I want
a share in every monied punter north of Carter Bar. I'll
feature on the Queen's New Year's Honours List for services
to the Scottish Tourist Industry. I'll make the biggest impact

on the balance of payments since North Sea oil and Westminster won't see a penny of it! I'll start in Edinburgh, where the money is, and work outwards . . . through Glasgow . . . Aberdeen . . . I'll establish a network of rent-boys from the Clyde shipyards to the Cairngorms . . . from the oil rigs to the Outer Hebrides . . . I'll sponsor orgies in bankrupt stately homes and fly in Concordes full of foreign punters. It'll be my turn to screw the fucking rent!

Robert   Piss off and have a bath. Richard'll come in and scrub your back.

Phil   Are you still my friend?

He goes into the bathroom.

Richard   Have you got the money you owe me?

Robert   Oh . . . not yet, Richard. Are you short?

Robert is affectionate again.

Richard   The spell is broken, Robert.

Outside the Golden Egg.

Eddie (*off*)   . . . and you can stuff your fucking eggs up your arse . . .

Eddie enters in his Golden Egg uniform.

I've chucked in my job at the Golden Egg. You can't fry fucking eggs with half your hand cut away. I'll fucking kill the bastard. Fucking knives is it now? I just want to get away from all this shit. Edinburgh isn't bloody worth it any more. All cities are rotten if you ask me . . . queer bastards after your money. I think I'd make a great gamekeeper. When I was visiting my granny in Newcastle I went off with this kid ferreting. He had this ferret. Just kept it in his jacket pocket. And we caught this bus . . . going after rabbits. You just stick them down this hole and the rabbits come flying out and you bash their bloody brains out with sticks. And I was standing there with this bloody great club and this thing comes belting out of the hole and I bloody hammered it and hammered it . . . and killed it . . . it was the ferret. I love animals.

Crawfords tea room.

Richard   There are times in a man's life when all he needs is a string quartet. Oh God . . . I need one now. I want to run away to my own warm fireside . . . with a cup of freshly made coffee . . . and listen to the Italian Quartet playing Beethoven's Opus 135 . . . but instead I've got to face up to the reality of poor Robert, (**Robert** *approaches the table with two coffees.*) who knows my time here is running out, and who wants to meet me straight from work at Crawfords.

Robert   Can I come back with you? To Newcastle . . . when you go back?

Richard   No.

Robert   Why not?

Richard   I like living alone.

Robert   Can't you give me a lift down? I'll find my own place to live. There's too many problems with Phil. It's like having the blood sucked out of you. Take me with you. Let me stay for a while . . . with you, Richard.

Richard   It's a rule I have about my life. Keep your own territory private. I've had people to stay. It doesn't solve anything. It just makes things more difficult. At the end of the day, people always end up by ripping me off one way or another.

Robert   I've brought you a present.

Richard   Oh . . .

Robert   Here. Take it.

Richard   Why?

Robert   Take it!

Richard *opens it. It's a lumber-jack shirt.*

Richard   . . . yes . . .

Robert   Will you wear it?

Richard   Yes.

Robert When you wear it, remember Robert from Edinburgh.

Robert *leaves.*

Eddie *is in the streets with a canvas bag full of personal belongings. One hand is bandaged.*

Eddie It's money really. I mean that's what it boils down to. I've washed my hand of Norma. She just uses me for money . . . that's all . . . and I don't like being used. She's a lost cause anyway. MacFerson's mother's got her fucking claws into her that deep. I'm leaving this city . . . but I'm not crawling out like some sort of rat. I'm leaving in style . . . first class by British Rail . . . so people will remember me. I'm going down to London. But Norma's cleaned me out again. And British Rail isn't fucking cheap. There's this guy I met when I was in the navy. He's a bouncer at this place in Greek Street. I phoned him up last night. He may be able to get me a job . . . you know . . . as a heavy. Just seeing that people behave and respect the law . . . at the club I mean. Keep the riff-raff out. I'll be ready to leave when I've sorted out my business here.

Later at the apartment.

Phil Write this down.

Robert I've no money.

Phil What's that got to do with it? This is money you owe.

Robert I can't pay it at the moment.

Phil Why not? What are you spending it all on? Coca-Cola?

Robert I'm saving.

Phil Ahh . . . we share this place. Gas . . . £34.70. Write it down. Electricity . . . £18.20. Now add it up . . . go on. I want you to know what it costs to run this place.

Robert £53.90.

Phil   What: £52.90. Don't make things worse. Divided by two. I said divided. Dear me . . .

Robert   I was away for five nights.

Phil   I don't care about your seamy private life. Divided by two . . .

Robert   It's not fair.

Phil   . . . a test of loyalty . . .

Robert   How can it be that much for gas?

Phil   What? Oh . . . some of last quarter's bill was passed on.

Robert   Last quarter? I wasn't here for last quarter. Right . . . that's half off the gas bill . . . £17.35. The rest of that is your problem. Plus £18.20. £25.55!

Phil   Rubbish. Are you trying to cheat me? Your friend?

Robert   Oh . . . £35.55. Right . . . half of that is . . . call it £18. I owe you £18. Is that fair?

Phil   Where's the money?

Robert   Close your eyes like a good boy. There you are. Magic.

Phil   I'll put it on the mantelpiece . . . and there's my contribution. Being an honest man, I concede you have a case concerning the extortionate gas bill. What's this? There's only £11 here. What about the other £7? You're trying to cheat me. *Me*!

Robert   I haven't got the rest just now. Can you wait till next week?

Phil   What are you doing with all your money? You've had some off that social worker . . . some off the Fire Brigade . . . and the Bank of Scotland . . .

Robert   . . . very little off the Bank of Scotland.

Phil   Get out on the streets. Take a trip to the Commonwealth Baths. Find a tourist. If you can't lay an American, retire! I want the money by tomorrow or you can fuck off out of here.

Robert Do you mean you want me to leave?

Phil You've got a little behind . . .

Robert I know . . .

Phil . . . with the rent.

The doorbell rings.

Robert Yours . . . sweetheart . . .

Phil *opens it.*

Eddie *knocks him to the floor and bursts in.*

Eddie I'm going to fix you!

Robert Christ!

Eddie (*to* **Robert**) Where are you going, son? Remember me?

Robert Don't touch me! I'll call the police.

Eddie It's him I want. That queer bastard.

Phil Who? Me? Eddie . . .

Eddie Trailing after us on a Saturday night . . .

Phil After you?

Eddie What's that money? I'll have that.

Robert Leave it alone.

Eddie How much is there here? Where is it?

He starts turning the place over. He opens a cupboard door and a load of baked bean tins falls on top of him.

Phil Why not try the bedroom?

Eddie I think I will. It was my idea! You didn't have to tell me. You're coming too.

Phil OK . . . OK . . . I'm coming.

Robert *takes his chance and escapes from the flat and locks the door from the outside.*

Eddie Where's the money then?

Phil There isn't any.

Eddie *pulls out the flick knife.*

Phil   Don't be mad! What would Norma say?

Eddie   Where's it hidden?

Phil   I told you. There isn't any. Robert's away for the police.

Eddie   What?

Phil   Get out while you can . . . and give me the money back.

Eddie   Fuck off. You paid me this to screw you . . .

Eddie *continues to turn the place over, discovering all sorts of equipment and porn mags.*

Phil   Haaa . . . the police would die laughing. I wouldn't be fucked by you . . . fucking fascist bastard. I detest you and your pansy little friends camping around Rose Street. Get out of here . . . you shit-hole.

Eddie   I only let Norma speak to me like that!

Phil *(aside)*   Where's the Special Branch when you need it?

Eddie   Cunt . . .

Eddie *finds the door of the apartment locked.*

Bastaaaaaarrrrrrds . . .

Phil   Haaaa . . . you're trapped. You'll never get out now. Give me the money back . . . quickly.

Eddie   Fuck offff . . . does that window open?

Phil   Yes . . . yes . . . climb out of the window.

Eddie   I thought of that!

Phil *opens the window.* **Eddie** *climbs out and sits on the ledge.*

Eddie   Christ! We're two floors up!

Phil   Jump, you coward . . . *jump!*

Eddie   I'll fucking kill myself!

Phil   Don't worry. They never cut the grass.

Eddie   I can't.

Phil   Use the drain pipe.

Eddie   Where?

Phil   There!

Phil *takes the money and the knife out of* **Eddie**'s *pocket and pushes him off the ledge.*

Eddie   AAAAAAHHHHHHhhhhh . . .

Phil *slams the window shut. The door is unlocked and* **Robert** *enters cautiously.*

Phil   Thanks, pal.

Robert   . . . what have you done with him?

Phil *points at the window.*

Robert   Liar . . .

Phil *waves the knife and the money at* **Robert**. **Robert** *opens the window and looks down.*

Eddie (*off*)   Bastaaaaaaaaaaaards . . .

Robert   Jesus!

Phil   Dear me . . . still living?

Robert   Ooooohhh . . . Phil . . .

Eddie (*off*)   Fucking queer cunts. We'll hunt you down you bastards. You'll never be safe again, Philip MacFerson . . . never . . . *never* . . . we'll cut you up, MacFerson. You're a dead man. You'll be fucking trampled on, you queer bastards . . .

Robert *shuts the window.*

Eddie   . . . trampled on . . .

Phil   How diverting.

Robert   What are we going to do?

Phil   What's new? The gutter's always been full of rats.

Robert   I'm going for the police.

Phil   What? Keep off my territory. I may have a word with my Vice Squad friends.

Robert   . . . got to do something . . .

Phil   Let's treat ourselves to new denim jackets . . .

Robert   *No!*

Phil   Yes.

Robert   Impossible.

Phil   Why?

Robert   . . . because I've hidden about twenty coat hangers in the cistern in the men's toilet. If I put any more in the bog'll never work and we'll really be in the shit.

Phil   OK . . . forget it. What a mess everything's in. Let's get things straight again . . . back to normal.

Robert   What's normal?

Phil   Like things were before.

Robert   That guy scared me!

Phil   Eddie? He's always like that.

Robert   I've had enough. That's it. I've paid my dues. I'm leaving.

Phil   When?

Robert   Now. I want somewhere I can relax . . .

Phil   Relax . . . relax. I'll make you some coffee.

Robert   It's too late. It's finished.

Phil   What are you going to do? Where are you going?

Robert   I don't know. Stop pestering me. You pester people! Did you know that?

Phil   Are you still my friend?

Robert   Leave me alone.

Phil   I want you here.

Robert   No.

Phil   Yes.

Robert   No.

Phil   Wait till the end of the week. We'll go to a party.

Robert *walks out.* **Phil** *is left alone with the money and the knife and the chaos. The door bell rings.* **Phil** *seizes the knife and stares at the door.*

Phil *approaches the door. The bell rings again. He opens it. His father is standing there with a hold-all.*

Mr MacFerson   I found out where you lived.

Phil   Come in, Da. How?

Mr MacFerson   I phoned through to that college.

Phil   Oh . . . yes . . .

Mr MacFerson   I suppose this is a surprise.

Phil   Yes.

Mr MacFerson   Sorry, son . . .

Phil   . . . not bothered.

Mr MacFerson   Sarah all right, is she?

Phil   She's fine. How's Jenny . . . Gavin . . . Hamish . . . Nicky . . .

Mr MacFerson   Oh . . . fine . . . Simon's had the measles.

Phil   Poor Simon.

Mr MacFerson   Sandra's doing her 'O' levels this summer.

Phil   Oh . . .

Mr MacFerson   . . . runs in the family . . .

Phil   What's that then?

Mr MacFerson   I was wondering if you would do us a favour, son.

Phil   Oh . . .

Mr MacFerson   Look after this.

Phil   What is it?

Mr MacFerson   Bits and pieces. It's got to stay out of the way for a while. I thought of you, Philip.

Phil   Yes.

Mr MacFerson   . . . never visited you here. I though I'd
call round and see if you could help. I needed someone I could
trust. Someone in the family.

Phil   Am I in the family?

Mr MacFerson   I thought of you, Philip. That's all.

Phil   Are you up to date with payments to Mother?

Mr MacFerson   Aye. Not quite. I will be when I've settled
this lot. Has she been complaining?

Phil   No. She never talks about you.

Mr MacFerson   No . . . well . . . can I rely on you then?

Phil   How long?

Mr MacFerson   Maybe a month or two. No hurry at the
moment. Let things cool off for a while. Will you do it, son?

Phil   You've got to the end of the month to settle up with
Mother.

Mr MacFerson   Oh Philip . . . don't interfere. I don't need
that. I only came to ask a wee favour. I thought it was about
time you and I got together a bit more. There's always . . .
things to work on. It might suit us both.

Phil   It might. But as far as I'm concerned, this is business.
Settle with Mother.

Mr MacFerson   You'll not got telling her about this.

Phil   No. I'll not interfere. Just sort things out in your own
way. Pay what's due. That's the price I'm asking for storage
space.

Mr MacFerson   Are you not pleased to see me?

Phil   Yes. But I told you. This is business. Do you agree?

Mr MacFerson   Not a word to your mother?

Phil   Agreed.

Mr MacFerson   Agreed. If you need to contact me there's
a number for you.

Phil   Right.

Mr MacFerson I'll be away now.

Phil I'll make you coffee.

Mr MacFerson No. I've other calls to make yet. (*He produces money.*) I was planning to give you this for doing it, but you've driven a harder bargain, you bastard. There's a future for you, son. I'll keep this for myself. You know there's a price to pay if anything happens to that stuff.

Phil Aye.

Mr MacFerson Take care now.

Phil You too. Call again sometime . . . now you've found us again . . .

Mr MacFerson Aye . . . maybe . . .

He goes. **Phil** *picks up the knife again, closes it and puts it in his pocket.*

Robert *is hitching by the roadside outside Edinburgh.*

Robert Come on . . . come on . . . Bastards! Thank God I've made a decision. With a bit of luck I'll be in Nottingham in a few hours. There's this kid down there. He's my age. We first met in the Turkish. I was laid out on this slab like a sweaty corpse. He was doing the massage. We never spoke. Then that night I spotted him at Shades . . . said hello. He said he didn't recognise me with my clothes on. One of them will stop. So I phoned this kid up an hour ago. He's expecting me. It's great to know that there's someone there . . . waiting for you . . .

Eddie, *bruised and bandaged, outside* **Norma**'s *apartment in Leith.*

Eddie Norma . . . *Norma* . . . I know you're up there. I'll come and knock your fucking door down if you don't let me in. Norma . . . *Norma* . . . you whore . . . I fucking need you. I'm hurt. I'm bruised all over . . . *and it wasn't my fault.* For Christ's sake . . . I need you . . . and I'm not fucking pissed. For God's sake open the fucking door.

Eddie *is soaked by a bucket of water.*

Ooooooohhhhhhhhhhhhhh Jesssssssussssss. Right. That's it you cunt. You're really out of my fucking life for good. Right *out*. That's absolutely fucking *it* . . .

Richard *has arrived back at his place in Newcastle.*

Richard   My home smells damp. It's amazing how things go stale when a home isn't lived in. The kitchen has always been bad, mind. I put up a false hardboard wall to cover one side of it. It looks fine at the moment, but I know there's trouble just out of sight. Maybe I'll put in electric storage heaters to keep the place aired when I'm away. They don't need anyone to be there.

I found that my Access card was missing on the way home. I stopped off to buy petrol. There was no money missing. Just the card itself. I can't really believe that Robert was responsible. I don't think he had a chance to take it. I may have lost it. I don't know. I've got it insured against loss anyway.

Robert was on my mind all the way home. I nearly said on my conscience. He was beautiful. I thought so. I'd love to have taken care of him. Made a home for him. Put him on his feet. There was no future in it. I've seen it all before. They stay a week or two, then you come back one evening and find a load of your things missing and they're away. What's the point of asking to be ripped off?

Perhaps Robert was different. Perhaps I've missed something of real value in my life.

I'm going to have a hot bath and listen to some music.

If only I was sure that he had real affection for me. Me as a person . . .

Anyway . . . it's finished.

Music: Mozart Divertimento played by the Italian Quartet, the presto finale of Divertimento KV 136.

Accounts

Accounts was first performed at the Traverse Theatre Club on 7 May 1981, with the following cast:

Mary Mawson	Madelaine Newton
Andy Mawson	Kevin Whately
Donald Mawson	Cliff Burnett
James Ridley-Bowes	David Calder
John Duff	Anthony Roper

Directed by Peter Lichtenfels
Designed by Andy Greenfield
Lighting by Colin Scott

At the Edinburgh Festival and at the Riverside Studios in 1981 the part of **James** was played by George Pensotti

The American première was at the Hudson Guild Theater, New York, on 1 June 1983, with the following cast:

Mary Mawson	Kathleen Nolan
Andy Mawson	Josh Clark
Donald Mawson	Kevin Conroy
James Ridley-Bowes	Allan Carlsen
John Duff	Frank Girardeau

Directed by Kent Paul
Designed by Jane Clark
Costumes by Mariann Verheyen
Lighting by Phil Monat

Part One

Autumn 1979

A farm in the Scottish Borders near Kelso.

Mary (*from her journal*)   Andy still cannot get used to Black-Face sheep. He's pining for Swaledales. I told him that it'll take time, but his heart will mend. Donald is still back at Dean Burn in spirit. He says he can hear his father's voice calling sheep on the fell top. Yet it's two full years since Harry was killed. The boys were saying last night that he'd travelled north with the family. This morning I drove the Landrover into Kelso for provisions. It's a fair-sized town, bigger than Allendale with great buildings and a fine bridge. Yetholm WI are having a poetry competition next time round. I'll write mine in my journal. The year's starting to close in on us . . .

Andy *and* **Donald** *on the fell top with their dogs, Gyp and Patch.*

Andy (*whistling instructions to his dog, then calling to his brother*)   Donald! . . . what's it like over by yon dyke?

Donald (*off*)   All clarts . . .

Andy   What?

Donald (*off*)   Clarty man.

Andy (*to his dog*)   Haaaaaaaaaaaaa . . . you rascal . . .

Donald (*off*)   Head them off . . . divven send them through here . . . (*Whistling.*)

Andy   Ahhhh Patch man . . . ah-ah-ah-ah . . .

Donald (*entering*)   What are you playin' at man? . . . Gyp . . . (*Whistling.*)

Andy   I thought yonder was a short cut.

Donald   Noooooo...

Andy   Hell... let them be a while... byyyyyyy... but that's a grand view. Is that the sea, Donald?

Donald   Aye... could be...

Andy   Wind's getting fierce...

Donald   ... and Kelso's doon there like... in that direction...

Andy   ... a canny distance...

Donald   Played against Tweed last season... with Hadrian colts... beat them... and in the Gala sevens...

Andy   And it's all ours...

Donald   What do you mean?... Just our bit's ours like...

Andy   No landlords... no rents... no agents putting up prices... hanging round your neck... Da would be pleased...

Donald   Da'd never have left Dean Burn...

Andy   ... never have left Swaledales... but these are wor fells...

Donald   Not wors till we growed wi'em a while... till we're hefted like the sheep...

Andy   ... wors in the bank...

Donald   We best drive 'em past yon rowan tree...

Andy   Howay...

Donald   It's ower clarty your way, man. We'll have to build ditches all over... it's useless there...

Andy and **Donald** *shelter from the wind by a stone wall. They drink from a thermos and eat their sandwiches.*

Donald   It's no use increasing the sheep till the drainage is done, now!

Andy   Maybe...

Donald   I'm right...

Andy   Now... do you want to hear my great idea?

Donald   Gan on...

Andy   I know you divven like cows...

Donald   Not that...

Andy   Hang on... now then... you know the Burn
Pastures...

Donald   Aye...

Andy   It looks all stony and useless...

Donald   It is...

Andy   Now if we were to clear that...

Donald   Waste of time...

Andy   Listen you! Now there's scope for increasing pasture
down there, like... more hay... or maybes plant some
beet...

Donald   Down there?

Andy   Aye... it's possible... now...

Donald   Topsoil's ower thin... Old Willie just had an
occasional sick beast there... nothing for us, like...

Andy   More feed would help if we're increasing the dairy
herd...

Donald   Who wants that?

Andy   I do... this is my farm as much as yours. There's a lot
of sense in a milking parlour.

Donald   Now we're getting down to it.

Andy   There's money in't. I could cope with many more
beasts with a parlour.

Donald   There's no sugar in this tea.

Andy   Canny windy up here, mind.

Donald   What were you up to last night?

Andy   Not a great deal . . .

Donald   Aye . . . but what?

Andy   Went doon the toon.

Donald   Kelso?

Andy   Aye.

Donald   Do you have to wake us up when you come in, like?

Andy   I couldn't get my trousers off. I was hopping around in the dark and I landed on one of your boots. There's lasses in Kelso.

Donald   Never!

Andy   It's a remarkable fact.

Donald   And bars?

Andy   Few of them too. I scored, like.

Donald   No doubt.

Andy   She was a canny age . . . but better than nawt. Nineteen's supposed to be your prime. I don't want to let it pass by.

Donald   Seventeen's your prime.

Andy   Oh aye . . . that's more than you'd know!

Donald   If you're coming in pissed each night, you best sleep in your own bedroom.

Andy   Too cold. Let's gan o'er to Hawick the neet.

Donald   Noooo . . . there's only one reason I gan there.

Andy   Are you packing in rugby at Hadrian?

Donald   I thought I could train at Tweed and travel to Hadrian for the games. I could, like. Pressure's on for me to make a switch. More future for me as a player in the Borders. No doubt about that. Playing for Tweed colts Saturday.

Andy   Is that settled then?

Donald   Aye . . . playing centre . . .

Andy (*calling his dog*) Gyp . . . Gyp! Have you seen that circle? Them stones yonder?

Donald Aye . . . a canny few about . . . ower past yon gill . . . beyond the dyke . . .

Andy Aye . . .

Donald Canny few grouse . . .

Andy You check the stone walls up to the end of the old Roman fort. I'll start at the sheep dip and cut right up the fellside. I'll meet you ower yonder.

Donald Right.

They exit in different directions.

At the farmhouse. **Mary** *talking to* **James Ridley-Bowes**.

James . . . so I've been disgracing myself around the flesh pots of Newcastle. Not really disgracing myself. Wondering whether I ought to. Wondering how to.

Mary Harry took me into town once when we were courting. We went to a film and then went dancing. They were all the wrong dances. Not traditional, like.

James Most evenings I get back and flop into a bath and lie there for hours. And by the time I've got myself something to eat and got the fire lit I don't really feel like going out. At my boarding school the two worst crimes were smoking and talking to girls in the town. Lying, cheating, beating up people smaller than oneself were more or less tolerated. But fags and tarts, if I may use those dreadful expressions, were not on!

Mary That's a long time ago, mind. Time now to set all that aside.

James Yes.

Mary We used to have these great matches in the yard. Harry and me taking on the two boys. Cricket and football. I was canny at cricket. We used to have to sweep the yard first,

mind. It was still awful messy. But the football was the worst.
Sometimes in the most freezing weather we'd break out of an
evening and fix up the lights and battle away for two hours or
more and end up all clarts from head to foot with bleeding
ankles and tempers flaring. It's a miss, like. Boys need a man.

James   Yes.

Mary   At least you'll not be coming to put up the rent from
now on. The boys will be sorry to miss you . . .

James   Oh . . . not to worry. I'll be seeing Donald at the
Rugby Club one way or another. We've started training, tell
him. Tell him Willie's dropped a stone on his foot stone-
walling . . . and Droop's been tossed by a bull. He's all right –
He says he feels like he did after the Hawick match last season.

Mary   James, I want you to know that you've been good for
Donald . . . for us.

James   Oh . . . well.

Mary   The boys were saying they'd not be seeing you so
often . . . not now, like.

James   I'd like to see you through the first year of the new
farm. There's a lot can go wrong.

Mary   So we want you to call back when you're up this way.
If you come this way.

James   I will.

Mary   Harry's death is still with us. The boys are full of
energy, but they lack all the wisdom of the land that Harry
took with him. We still need a man around the place . . . at
times.

James   Well . . . I've got clients near Belford I've got to see
before getting back to Ponteland.

Mary   They say it'll take at least two years before the
phone's in.

James   Thanks for the coffee and cakes.

Mary   You're welcome.

James Well . . . goodbye . . .

Mary Goodbye . . .

Mary (*from her journal*) I seem to be losing touch with the folk from Allendale already. It's difficult for me to travel south to Northumberland to see them all. There's no telephone here and it's miles to the nearest call box. Secretly, I wonder if I'll ever settle here. It's for the boys, all this buying and moving . . .

John Duff, *the colts' coach at Tweed RFC, is on the phone to* **James Ridley-Bowes**, *the colts' coach of Hadrian RFC.*

Duff How many pitches are you using this year?

James Same as last . . . but we're keeping the sheep away from the one down by the river this season . . . one of our lads . . . Skittle . . . was sent off last year for throwing sheep shit at Durham's full back.

Duff You need to crack the whip a bit, James. Hadrian colts are a wild bunch of hooligans.

James At least we don't steal sheep.

Duff So the dates in our letter stand, do they?

James Yes. We look forward to slaughtering Tweed after our triumph of last year.

Duff In all that wind, rugby was hardly playable. It wasn't a game at all, James.

James We train our lads to play in all weathers.

Duff Talking of your lads, now . . . let's get down to business.

James Yes.

Duff We've been approached by one of your lads.

James Donald Mawson.

Duff   Aye. Now he wants to train with us but seems unclear in his mind whether he should be on our books or yours.

James   We still think of him as one of us.

Duff   No doubt. I remember him from last year. He caught the eye. There may be something there.

James   We think so.

Duff   I mean more than ordinary colts material. It depends on how he grows, how he develops. And the sort of coaching he receives.

James   Are you suggesting that he'll do better in the Borders than in Northumberland?

Duff   Of course he will, James! How could you doubt it?

James   I see. Carry on.

Duff   If we're going to coach him, which is what he has asked . . . he approached us first, remember . . . we would want to play him as well. Maybe not in our senior colts . . . unless he made it on merit. No special favours for the lad.

James   He'll have to make his own mind up. That's all there is to it.

Duff   Aye, that's right. I just don't want you to think we've been poaching.

James   I know you haven't . . . in this case. He could still travel down to us on a Saturday.

Duff   It's not fair on the lad. If he's going to be one of us, he better commit himself the whole way. He's got to decide for himself.

Donald *is stretched out at the farmhouse.* **Mary** *is setting the table for tea, which is a substantial meal.*

There's a blast of a shotgun, both barrels, from the yard. The rooks scream.

Mary   Dear God!

Donald   Andy's having a bit of a blast.

Andy *comes in with a shotgun.*

Mary   Warn us, will you!

Andy   Rooks divven give ne warning.

Donald   She said us, idiot.

Andy *points the gun at* **Donald** *and pretends to pull the trigger.*

Andy   Pow! Pow!

Mary   Never point guns!

Donald   Howay.

Andy   Empty.

Mary   Give me that.

Andy   I'm going to clean it. Leave it alone, man!

Mary   Father's gun that!

Andy   Mine now!

Donald   And mine.

Andy   Shurrup, you bairn!

Donald   Piss off!

Mary   I told you!

Andy   My baby brother hasn't learnt how to pull the trigger yet!

Donald   I'll wrap this poker round youse!

Andy   Mam . . .

Mary   What?

Andy   Has the *Hexham Courant* come yet?

Mary   When it does, it's me that reads it first . . . just like the old days.

Donald   Oooo . . . hark at her.

Andy   She's entering the nag of the month competition.

Mary Do you want your tea in here or flung out in the yard?

Andy Flung out in the yard please. No ... no ... I meant in here! Mam's getting sprightly.

Mary Be your age.

Andy I am. I'm being nineteen as hard as I can. Not always easy out here.

Donald You're right there, son.

Andy All right for you ... you're still into sheep. I want something better.

Mary What are you two on about?

Donald Not got into Black-Face sheep.

Andy I should hope not.

Donald Blackies are thick ...

Andy They are, like.

Donald Some angles your head's the same shape as a Blackie.

Andy You child!

Mary I've been working on my poem.

Donald What poem?

Mary For the Women's Rural Institute.

Andy Gan on. Let's hear it.

Mary Donald's been writing one as well.

Andy Donald?

Mary Aye.

Donald No need to tell him!

Andy I didn't know he could write.

Mary Read it out.

Andy Let's hear it.

Donald No! It hasn't had the finishing touches yet.

Andy Finishing touches! No time for them. Read it!

Donald No!

Andy Gi'us it!

Donald Gerroff man! Ahhhhhh . . .

Andy (*reading the poem that he's snatched*) 'I love to walk the soddin' fells . . .'

Mary Is that what it says?

Donald (*snatching it back*) Give me that!

Andy ' . . . soddin' fells . . . ' What's one of them, like?

Donald ' . . . sodden fells . . . ' It means they're wet, you ignorant worm.

Mary What's the rest of it?

Andy Something about 'dingly dells' . . .

Donald What lies!

Andy And sheep that 'fall down wells' . . .

Mary Sheep don't fall down wells.

Donald Billy Ferguson had one that did! It was a Swaledale!

Andy Of course it was! All Billy's are, you creep. If they'd been Blackies the whole lot would have fallen down the bloody well.

Mary Language!

Donald You can all hear my poem when it's finished!

Mary And mine.

Andy (*producing a piece of paper from his pocket*) And mine!

Duff *is at Tweed RFC on the phone to his wife.* **James** *is at Hadrian RFC phoning his colts.* **Duff** *is drinking whisky.* **James** *is drinking beer.*

Duff   I'm sorry . . . there's a committee meeting on . . .
Helen, I know you've got supper ready . . . I know it's unfair of
me, but you know how important this is . . . I know duckling *à
l'orange* is important too . . . of course you're not a widow . . .

James   Hello Mrs Westerby . . . is John there, please? . . .
hello, Snot . . . how are you? You played well last week . . . well
I thought you did . . . I know you dropped an absolutely vital
pass . . . Studs should have passed sooner . . . it was his fault
rather than yours . . . now you mustn't let it get you down,
Snotty . . . it's Stud's problem . . . don't tell him that, of
course . . .

Duff   OK . . . OK . . . we'll make it four cans of lager . . .
bottles . . . right . . . four bottles of lager . . . four plain crisps . . .
Look, there's no lasses here, just big brute rugby players . . .
Mavis might just as well be a big brute rugby player. Helen,
I've got to drive to Aberdeen tonight to pick up some
fertiliser. I've got to be back here for tomorrow's match! . . .

James   Hello . . . Studs? . . . Ahhhh . . . now then, are you fit
for training tomorrow night? . . . That was just a scratch,
man! . . . What? . . . A great tough thing like you? . . . What's
the matter? . . . Well get it cut short then they'll not be able to
swing you round by it! . . . That was Snot's problem . . . he's
never been good with his hands . . . You could have released
the ball a couple of strides earlier . . . But you must come to
training . . . tell her that you'll see Clint Eastwood on Friday
night . . . Well that's too bad . . . she knew your Wednesday
nights were booked before she started going out with you . . .
be tough, Studs . . . don't be bossed around . . . What do you
mean 'it's all right for me to talk'? . . .

Andy *has met up with* **Donald**, *who has been training, in the streets of
Kelso.*

Andy   It's only half-past nine.

Donald   Look! I've had a drink at the club.

Andy   Why mannnn . . . take a look around the town.

Donald No! Let's go home!

Andy I'm not ready to.

Donald It takes an hour to get back. We've an early start in the morning. Market's tomorrow.

Andy I know that, young'un. There's folks I'm wanting to meet yet.

Donald Why mannnn . . . you've been on the town all night! You're reeking! I'll be driving you.

Andy You? You've not passed your test, son.

Donald You're not fit.

Andy It's me that's pickin' youse up the night. Anyways . . . I was hoping to happen on a lass.

Donald Ahhhh mannn . . . there's ne time for that.

Andy Doesn't take long.

Donald You're like a whippet . . . whip it in and whip it out.

Andy Maybe there's something for you.

Donald Like what?

Andy Like her daughter.

Donald Daughter! Who is this? Have you been breaking into the old people's home?

Andy No!

Donald I thought you said it was a lass you were after.

Andy She's nearly a lass.

Donald So was Queen Victoria. How old is't?

Andy Thirties maybes. You don't want to be that personal when you're screwing the arse off someone.

Donald So why divven you gan wi'hor?

Andy Mother kind of shoves her out of the way, like. Ahhh mannnnnnnn, do you not fancy it?

Donald Whyyyyyy . . . Maybe . . .

Andy   Come on then.

Donald   No!

Andy   We're wasting time.

Donald   Not with you there . . . I couldn't.

Andy   I divven want to watch you wi'hor. I'll be busy.

Donald   Not with your own brother. No, I couldn't. That would be in . . . in . . . inthingy.

Andy   We sleep in the same bed at home.

Donald   That's different. We're used to that, like.

Andy   You are horny, aren't you?

Donald   Shurrup man . . . they'll hear you.

Andy   My brother's got a horn on!

Donald   I'll bray youse!

Andy   Oooooo . . .

Donald   Where's the bloody Landrover?

Andy   Ah-haaaaa . . .

Donald   I'll fuck youse!

Andy   Catch us first, little big horn!

Donald *brings* **Andy** *down and slaps his face.* **Andy**'s *surprised at his strength but shakes himself free.*

Andy   Watch it, you!

Donald   Let's gan!

Andy   No.

Donald   Give us the keys then.

Andy   No way!

Donald   You stay on . . . I'll go home. I'll pick you up early.

Andy   At yon corner?

Donald   Aye.

Andy Don't tell Mam.

Donald No.

Andy *tosses him the keys.*

Donald Where is't?

Andy Beyond yon bridge end.

Donald Half-five?

Andy I've no watch . . . aye . . . half-five . . . or you could do the cows and make it half-eight? That would save you getting up so early. I'll make it up, like.

Donald Right . . . eight-thirty.

Andy . . . and Nellie's got an ulcer . . .

Donald . . . right . . .

Andy . . . and Maggie's got the shits!

Donald Behave now!

Andy Who me? Of course.

They split.

Some days later in Kelso.

Mary *is carrying a load of shopping back to her Landrover. She is approached by* **Duff**.

Duff Mrs Mawson . . .

Mary Yes . . .

Duff Can I help you carry that?

Mary I'm managing . . .

Duff I'm John Duff . . .

Mary Oh . . .

Duff I run the Tweed colts . . .

Mary Oh aye . . . Donald said . . .

Duff I wanted to talk to you . . .

Mary   About Donald?

Duff   Aye.

Mary   He's keen.

Duff   Aye . . . we know that . . .

Mary   What do you want to tell me, Mr Duff?

Duff   I . . . well . . . we hope you're settling in . . . that's it . . .
he's a good lad . . . we want him to settle . . . with us . . . we
might be able to make something of him . . . out of the
ordinary . . . if he sticks with us . . . I'm in the fertiliser
business . . . if you want to get in touch . . . there's my home
number . . .

Mary   Donald has it . . .

Duff   Are you in the Women's Rural Institute?

Mary   Aye.

Duff   I tell ghost stories! I get all dressed up for it!

Mary *exits towards her Landrover.*

Duff *follows.*

On the fell **Andy** *and* **Donald** *are carrying bales of hay on their backs
to feed the sheep. Although they're exhausted, they sing as they trudge out
of sight across the fell top.*

Winter 1979

Mary (*from her journal*)   We have now been living on our new
farm for three full months. So far we've been spared the worst
of an early winter, which is a blessing in these parts. I think of
our farm as being long, with high fells and the sheep, and low
pastures with just a few beasts. Andy wants to increase the
dairy side of things. The last farmer couldn't cope with that,
although the potential was there. Andy says that with a
milking parlour he can cope with many more beasts himself.

The wind has a different sound and feel to it here. I mean compared to our old home in Dean Burn in the Allen Valley. We are high here, more out-by. The wind sings with a sharper voice. It was blowing a gale the other night. Things kept falling off the inside of the slate roof onto the ceiling above my bed. Maybe the roof wants working on.

James *is visiting* **Mary Mawson**.

James   You must make sure that there isn't a cash flow crisis in six months' time. That's the trick.

Mary   I know. We're planning on carrying a few more sheep. We're not exactly overstocked.

James   A good idea.

Mary   And the boys are on about clearing what we call the Burn Pastures. That's down by the river beyond the first gate.

James   I know . . . that's . . . ha . . . always been a problem. Old Willie stuck a sick beast in there occasionally.

Mary   They think it's wasted at the moment. Maybe they could plant out some beets or maybe a barley crop.

James   Yes . . . oh dear . . . look . . . it's too stony . . . for the work involved . . . it's hardly worth it.

Mary   It was just an idea, like.

James   Donald has deserted us.

Mary   Aye. I'm sorry.

James   We could have done with him this season.

Mary   Tweed's a lot more convenient.

James   It's a pity.

Mary   It's nawt to do with me, now. Donald is his own boss . . . except in the house.

James   Yes . . . right.

Mary   And Andy wants to increase the dairy herd . . . get one of these new milking parlours.

James   I see.

Mary   The byres will convert easy enough. With Andy taking care of beasts and Donald away with the sheep, the boys'll not get under each other's feet. It's almost two farms in one, James.

James   You're planning an additional bank loan for the milking parlour?

Mary   Aye.

James   The fixed interest rate is a blessing, Mary, but don't overdo it.

Mary   I've always been a good accountant in the past.

James   True.

Mary   The boys have a long time ahead of them. We must plan.

James   Look, I hope you don't think I'm stepping out of turn . . .

Mary   No.

James   If you feel unsure or worried about how things are going, talk to someone right away. Don't set things to one side. You've got to deal with problems at once. Forgive me, Mary. I'm interfering.

Mary   We need your advice.

Andy *is on the telephone – a pay phone.*

Andy   Hello? . . . Mrs Duff? Andy Mawson here. Aye . . . that's the one . . . I know I shouldn't . . . Howay . . . I had to phone you, like . . . couldn't help it . . . Is that miles out-by by any chance? . . . I've had some sleep . . . aye . . . about three hours . . . I know I'm not behaving myself . . . I know . . . it's more fun being bad . . . you know that . . . I didn't mean exactly that, like . . . I didn't mean it . . . No . . . honest . . . I'm sorry . . . look . . . I'm sorry . . . of course I gan to church . . . what's that got to do with it? . . . right . . . you're right . . . I'm

driving ower to Hawick this afternoon . . . I've got problems
with my distributor . . . no I'm not going to the clinic . . . the
distributor on the tractor . . . well you shouldn't read all these
women's magazines . . . it's only townies get that, like . . .
now . . . shall I look by? . . . It's ne risk if he's miles out-by . . .
Of course I'll make it snappy . . . if you want it snappy you can
have it snappy, Mrs Duff . . . right . . . see . . .

She has hung up suddenly.

Down at Tweed Rugby Club. **John Duff** *in his track suit. He has
taken* **Donald**, *all muddy and sweaty, on one side.*

Duff You . . . aye . . . you Mawson . . . here lad! How many
games has it been now? How many?

Donald Seven or eight.

Duff You don't know exactly, Mawson?

Donald Not exactly.

Duff Now listen, laddie. You're holding the ball too long,
like the Hadrian lads. You're part of Tweed now . . .
remember? You cannot expect to barge your way through.
The lads really tackle up here. None of your fancy Hadrian
Academical stuff. When you get the ball in the centre say to
yourself 'Can I make ten yards?' If you can't, pass it out
straight away . . . in a flash . . . no hesitating. Now Fergus on
the wing has a fair bit of pace . . . at least as much as you,
Donald son. If he scores, you've scored because you've been
part of that movement. And up here we don't like to see our
wingers getting frozen and see the ball only twice in a match.
Wingers are for using at Tweed . . . and if you get in the way of
that you'll find yourself running the touch in no time . . . tries
or no tries . . . Is that clear? Now what have you got to do?

Donald Get the ball out . . . unless I can make ten yards . . .

Duff Good! For your reward! *Ten press-ups.*

Donald *is down in a flash doing his press-ups.*

Duff   One two three four . . . that's it . . . seven eight nine . . .
up on your feet . . . *down again* . . . five for luck . . . one two three
four five . . . *get up!* Now here's the second thing. Once you've
moved the ball out, I want you to run round to support
Fergus . . . aye . . . miss out the other centre occasionally like
you did tonight . . . that was good, Donald. Young Willie will
cover for you. You're vital to us, Donald . . . creating the
overlap . . . running all over . . . you've got a future if you do
what you're told. Understand laddie?

Donald   Aye.

Duff   I'll be watching you specially on Saturday. *Touch your
toes!* One two three four five . . . Now away to your bath . . .
run! And keep it simple! . . . *Hey Scottie . . . bring in those posts . . .
no . . . the other ones . . . aye . . . no . . .* Jesus!

At the farm, **Mary** *has cornered* **Andy**. *He is studying the plans for the
milking parlour.*

Mary   There's no way we can afford another vehicle.

Andy   He'll pass his test soon. Hell! He drives the
Landrover more than I do. Coppers'll get him one of these
days.

Mary   I'm going to put a stop to all that too. It's about time
someone put their foot down in this house.

Andy   Howay and see the plans for the milking parlour.

Mary   What do you think I've been looking at all day? And
don't try changing the subject, Andrew Mawson.

Andy   What subject?

Mary   You know what's on my mind.

Andy   Really?

Mary   Do you think I haven't heard about your carrying
on?

Andy   What do you mean?

Mary   The women were full of it. Talking away when they though I was out of ear-shot.

Andy   What were they saying, like?

Mary   Unrepeatable things! About other folk's wives . . .

Andy   Just a bunch of old gossips. I don't know why you bother with them.

Mary   You'll land my family in trouble before you're through. Can you not stick to courting like the other young men do?

Andy   What other young men are you on about? Nawt different about me. Maybes I'm a little more imaginative than some . . .

Mary   That's the least of it from what I hear. And it's affecting the farm . . . and us . . .

Andy   How's that?

Mary   Milking the cows later and later.

Andy   It always gets done.

Mary   And all this talk of raising another £50,000 for the milking parlour . . .

Andy   It's done! Bank's agreed the principle at least. Things just need signing.

Mary   You'll get no signature from me the way you're carrying on.

Andy   You'll benefit too. You know the money side of things. You said it was canny enough when we all discussed it.

Mary   Only if we get enough back from the increased milk yield to pay off the loan. It's getting things balanced that matters. It's risks like we've never faced before. Risks of not paying rent as tenants but owning things with none to bail you out if things slip. And you're playing about as though you owed nothing to anyone. Father would have whipped you and thrown you out by now!

Andy   Like hell he would!

Mary His insurance money and the compensation is all tied up in the loans. Remember that! We may own a farm now but we've no cash to speak of. So end this talk of new cars.

Mary *leaves in distress.* **Andy** *follows her.*

Andy We want the milking parlour!

Donald *and* **James** *are together in Kelso finishing fish and chips.*

James Duffer's been doing well . . . scored twice against Percy Park.

Donald Aye.

James . . . and Pud's still getting into trouble. He will allow himself to get so worked up. They all know about him . . . the opposition . . . and they work on him on purpose . . . just trying to get himself sent off or something daft. We had this lady referee the other week and all the lads were frightfully well behaved. They couldn't stand the idea of getting ticked off by a mere woman. But Pud just did the same old business . . . scrapping away in the loose mauls.

Donald He's thick.

James She gave him such a dressing-down. Pud just stood there . . . shell-shocked. God! He was absolutely useless for the rest of the game. We had to take him off! Poor Pud.

Donald I miss the lads, like.

James Get yourself down sometime. They keep asking after you.

Donald Aye.

James You're looking fit.

Donald Aye. Training's hard up here, mind.

James If you decide you've had enough at the end of the season, you can always come back to us.

Donald I'm taking my driving test Tuesday. I'll be getting a car sometime . . . driving legally soon, like. Do you want us back?

James Yes.

Donald I mean . . . you personally? Have you missed us?

James Yes.

Donald I'm not yet settled, James. I still think myself back to Dean Burn. Things is different here. The air. The fells. The wind. It tires you more than it did at home . . . harder somehow. Winter's been canny mild, mind.

James Plenty of hay in?

Donald Enough. Maybe more than enough if it carries on the way it's going. It's good, like. But on the fells it's ower boggy . . . marshy, like . . . and it's easy to get lost when the mist comes down. And your instincts don't take you home some nights. Not straight away. We're not with the land yet, James. It's hard.

James You and Andy should get your own two-way radios . . .

Donald No. We don't do things like that, James.

James Is there anywhere round here I can have a pee?

Donald There's a canny wall round there.

James I don't think I should.

Donald The river's a walk off, but it would take no harm . . . even with a bladder like yours.

James Look . . . oh . . . well . . . keep a look out . . . whistle if anyone's coming . . .

James *goes to pee.* **Donald** *screws up his chip paper and lobs it like a grenade, whistling as it flies through the air.*

James (*rushes back*) God . . . I can't see anyone . . . bloody hell . . . I've pissed all down my leg?

Donald I didn't mean to whistle . . . it just kind of came out!

James   I'm bursting! Help!

Donald   Come on with me. I'll show you where.

James   Hurry.

Donald   Tie a knot in it.

James   We might never get it undone!

Donald   *We?*

Duff *is telling stories to the Women's Rural Institute. He is dressed like a Borders character from a Sir Walter Scott novel.*

Duff   . . . now Billy Macrae lived at Glen Cune and he was the meanest man in the valley. He never settled his bills. He was never known to give gifts at any time of the year, even to Old Tilly, his wife. And folks couldn't understand how Old Tilly had stood for all her husband's cruelty all those years. And they grew old together, and yet he still would beat her with his stick when he fell into one of his foul moods. Now I'll tell you the strange things that happened.

One day, Tilly was away in the wood gathering sticks. And it was a dark day with the north wind blowing. And she thought she heard a voice. 'Tillllllllyyy . . . Tillllllllyyy . . . pick them berries . . . the berries by yon mountain ash . . . ' And she straightened her aching back to look around. But there was no soul to be seen! And there by the mountain ash she saw the deadly nightshade gleaming!

And Billy Macrae . . . he died that week. There was no money for his funeral and they buried him in the darkest, dankest spot in Studholm Churchyard. And within the year, a mountain ash grew out of Billy's grave and folk said its roots were feeding on Billy's bones and it was his only generous act in a long black life! And the tree is still there to be seen!

And Old Tilly lived another twenty years and folk said they'd never seen her so happy.

And we know why . . . good ladies . . .

Spring 1980

Mary (*from her journal*)   Spring's setting in early this year.
The weather's been exceptionally mild. One of my new
excitements at Comb Law is discovering what there is
planted in the garden round the house. There's been
snowdrops all over, sometimes packed so close that bulbs
have been forced out of the ground by their neighbours. These
I've gathered carefully and redistributed. It's a wonder that
bulbs so freshly planted have the energy to flower so quickly.
There's been an abundance of crocuses. The trouble was
avoiding treading them down by accident. And there's been a
shrub bursting cherry pink with colour that caught me
entirely by surprise. The flowers have come before the leaves
and seemed, on the cold morning that I found it in bloom, to
be a miracle.

The new milking parlour is all but finished with the mild
weather.

There has been sad news from nearby. A tractor overturned
and crushed the lad from the next valley. Strangely, his
grandfather died in the same spot in similar circumstances
many years back . . .

One evening at the farmhouse. **Andy**'*s busy with the* Farmers'
Weekly. **Mary** *comes in to get the table prepared for tea.*

Mary   Do you want feeding or not?

Andy   'Corse!

Mary   Shift yourself then.

Andy   Oh Mammmmm!

Mary   Over to the sofa! Howay!

Andy *shifts.* **Donald** *enters all mucky from the byre with his boots
still on.*

Mary   Out of here with your boots all clarting the place up!

Donald   Oh aye.

He leaves.

Andy   Where's the embrocation, Mam?

Mary   What do you want that for?

Andy   My thigh's playing war.

Mary   It's over by the coal bucket where Donald left it last time.

Mary *goes back to the kitchen.*

Andy *fetches the embrocation, drops his jeans by the fire and rubs some on his thigh.* **Donald** *comes back with his boots off.*

Donald   That's mine, man!

Andy   Took a bit of a tumble the day, like.

Donald   Don't use any more. I need that.

Donald *takes the bottle. He pours some on his hand.*

You divven want to get this near your balls. You catch fire!

Andy   Mine catches fire without that, like.

Donald *suddenly attempts to get the hand with the embrocation inside* **Andy**'*s pants.*

Andy   Howay. You bent bastard! Get stuffed you! You poof!

Mary *comes in.*

Mary   What are you playing at? Disgusting! I'm not standing for it!

Andy   He's been queer all day, him.

Donald   Get lost!

Andy   Something's up.

Donald   Aye ... something is!

Mary   Get decent the pair of you! (*She goes out.*)

Andy *gets back to the sofa with his* Farmers' Weekly.

Donald *slips a book out from his overalls and tries to read it privately.*

Andy What's that then?

Donald What?

Andy The book, man.

Donald Nothing much.

Andy Let's have a look.

Andy *manages to get the book off* **Donald**.

Donald Get lost you!

Andy Hey lad! How sly can you get? *The Swaledale Flock Book*!

Donald Give it here!

Andy Where did you get this?

Donald Borrowed it.

Andy Who off?

Donald None of your business! A friend!

Andy What friend's this?

Donald Give it here!

Mary (*off*) Stop shouting!

Andy Who lent it you, like?

Donald James.

Andy Oh aye. So you've been hiding it.

Mary *comes in.*

Mary What's this racket then?

Andy Donald's been hiding the *Flock Book* so he can have it first.

Donald Mam, tell him to give us it.

Andy *is reading it.* **Mary** *snatches it.*

Andy I was reading that!

Donald I was first!

Andy   You're all schemes and plans you. Sly . . . a sly brother!

Donald   Can I have it, Mam?

Mary   I want to have a look.

Donald   Tea's burning!

Mary   Help!

She rushes to the kitchen. The book is flung onto a chair and falls to the ground. Both brothers dive for it and they start to fight over it.

Donald   Fight you for it!

Andy   Cumberland wrestling rules!

Donald   Right!

They fight.

Andy   Bastard!

Donald   You fart!

Andy   Bloodly little turd!

Donald   You smelly sock!

Andy   Y-front!

Donald   Snot!

Andy   Acne!

Donald   Ahhhh . . . that's my arm . . . ahhhhh!

Andy   Is it really? How insignificant . . . how worthless . . .

Donald   Ahhhhh . . . ahhh man!

Donald *manages to get out of it and ends up on top of* **Andy***, with* **Andy** *flat on his back with his arms trapped.*

Donald   Divven move or I'll gob on you!

Donald *starts to trickle spit out of his mouth and then sucks it back just as it is about to fall on* **Andy***'s face.*

Andy   Don't . . . ahhhh . . . gob-shite . . . ahhhhhhh!

Donald *lets the dribble go too far and* **Andy** *has to take it in the face.*

Donald It's raining ... raining ...

Andy I'll get you ... ahhh ...

Donald Oh dear ... you're getting wet ...

Mary *comes in.*

Mary Get up the pair of you ... *get up!*

They get up.

Andy I'll not forget that ... you shit.

Mary I'll not have that word in my house!

Donald It's usually me underneath you, isn't it. Things are changing now. My turn now!

Mary Fighting and carrying on at each other's throats! I'll not take this from either of you!

Donald It's not me ... it's him!

Mary *clouts him.*

Mary Now sit down!

Andy Hee-heeee ...

Mary *clouts* **Andy.**

Mary And you!

The boys sit down obediently at the table.

Mary Now I think we'll have grace.

Andy Oh Mam ...

Donald What is it?

Mary Hands off! Liver hotpot ...

Andy Ugh!

Mary Shurrup!

Donald Shurrup Mam ... I'm prayin' ... Dear God ... thanks for Mam's stew ...

Andy ... it's hotpot ...

Donald ... and for my queer brother ...

Mary   Donald!

Donald   . . . and help me to recognise chronic liver fluke infestation when I see it!

Mary   That wasn't very nice.

Donald   Amen!

Andy   Amen!

Donald   Say amen, Mam.

Mary *serves out the food.*

Mary   Cut the bread please, Andrew.

Donald   Ooooo . . . Andrew!

Andy   Bonny-bum-Donny . . .

Donald   Sling ower the bread!

Andy   Hey lad! Is that all I get?

Donald   Pepper . . . pass the pepper!

Mary   Pass your mother the salt please, Donald.

Donald   There you are.

Andy   There's the pepper, Mam.

Donald   Do you want some bread?

Andy   There's the butter like . . .

Mary   Don't rush it! Eat it slow!

Donald   I'm starving.

Andy   I'm ravenous.

Donald   He's always stuffing something . . .

Andy *gets out* The Swaledale Flock Book.

Donald   Swaledales! You best get into Blackies, Andy lad.

Andy   I'd love to start Swaledales on these fells.

Donald   Canny expensive . . . take years . . . hefting them from one generation to another . . . building up the flock . . .

Mary And it's not just the sheep that stray till they're hefted. I know what's gannin' on. And we'll have no reading at table!

Andy There's no harm in't. I'm going to hold up a photo of one of the tups and I want you to guess what price it fetched at auction.

Mary Put that away!

Andy Father used to do this each year!

Andy *holds up one of the photos of a tup, covering up the details with his other hand.*

Andy How much? . . . howay . . . how much?

Donald £800 . . .

Andy Mam?

Mary Not at table.

Andy Gan on.

Donald Gan on, Mam.

Mary Errrr . . . £660 . . .

Andy Not bad . . . Donald's got it . . . £800 . . . What about this'un?

Donald Hold it closer . . . errrrrrr . . . £1350 . . .

Mary £500 . . .

Donald I'm good me, you know.

Andy How do you do it, lad? You're bang on again . . . £1350!

Donald I look at the wellies.

Andy Tups divven wear wellies, man!

Donald Noooo mannnn. In the pictures there's the wellies of him that's holdin' tup . . . and those are Eddie Pemberton's wellies and I remember the sale and it went to Colonel Netherton's farm out by Lazenby for £1350. Owerpriced in my opinion. That tup couldn't screw a yow if it tried!

Andy   My legs are aching something rotten.

Donald   And have you got sores in your mouth and is your nose running?

Mary   Send for the vet! Sit down you two! There's more to come yet.

Andy   What is't?

Mary   Jelly.

Donald   I love jelly.

Andy   I hate it!

Donald   I'll have yours.

Andy   Noooo . . . I'll eat it.

Mary (*serving it out*)   Get on then before it melts.

Andy   Jelly doesn't melt . . .

Donald   . . . it kind of wobbles to death.

Mary   Donald! Your hands are filthy!

Donald   They were clean a minute ago.

Andy   He's filthy all over, him!

Donald   Shurrup!

Mary   Hold your tongue!

Andy (*holding his tongue with his fingers*)
EEERRRRRRRRRRRRRR . . .

Donald *flicks a spoonful of jelly right into* **Andy**'s *face.*

Donald   Haaaaa . . .

Andy   Pig!

Mary   Stop it!

Andy *picks up a handful of jelly and flings it at* **Donald**.

Andy   I'll kill you!

Mary   Sit down!

Donald (*who is at the other side of the room*) Truce! I declare a truce!

Andy Well I don't!

Mary Sit down and finish your meal.

Andy Come here, Donald!

Donald On one condition!

Andy Oh aye.

Donald If I come back to the table and try to finish my jelly, do you promise to leave us alone?

Andy Gan on then.

Donald No . . . no . . . I want a promise. Do you swear?

Andy I promise I'll let you finish your jelly.

Donald You heard that everyone?

Donald *goes back to the table.*

Now then . . . please note that I'm going to eat most of my jelly but I'm going to leave just a little bit 'cos Andy said there was a truce till I'd finished my jelly BUT I'm *not going to finish it*! Is that clear?

Andy I've not forgotten that now.

Donald That's good.

Mary I think I'll clear the table.

Andy Let it be. I've not finished yet.

Donald Neither have I. In fact there's things I want to say.

Andy What things?

Donald Thoughts I've been having.

Andy Thoughts?

Donald Now you've got your milking parlour.

Andy Gan on then.

Donald We could be making more money.

Mary We need to!

Andy How, like?

Donald We're still not using our resources. If you've got resources it's daft not to use them.

Andy Parlour's using our resources.

Donald If the milk yield stays high enough ... aye ...

Andy Well then?

Donald There's tourism.

Andy Howay to hell!

Donald There's grants to be had. James was telling us.

Mary James.

Donald There's folk that want to visit the Borders. We could improve our property using other buggers' money. We can't keep raising loans. It's thousands more with the parlour to pay off.

Andy It pays for itself, idiot.

Donald The Nicholsons of Hartley Shield made about £10,000 doing almost nothing with bed-and-breakfasts and such like.

Mary Almost nothing! Workin' her fingers to the bone more likely!

Andy And folk trampling over their property ... their dogs frightening the sheep.

Donald The Burn Pastures has beaten us! We wasted days slogging away trying to clear the rocks and that. We'll never make awt out of that unless we use our heads. We'd best leave it as it is and get planning for a camp site ... maybes a caravan park. Why mannnn ... it's out of sight of us, isn't it? And the extra money would be useful at the tup sales. We're hill farmers at heart ... not dairymen. It's sheep we know about. And the cash would be useful for other things. We need a new Landrover.

Mary   We're not affording another Landrover and there's an end of it!

Donald   If we don't exchange it soon it'll not be worth anything, and prices is soaring!

Andy   What are tourists going to come here for?

Donald   Because we advertise. Pony trekking. Fishing.

Andy   Why mannn . . . they're just tiddlers, man.

Donald   There'll be more grants maybes for stocking the river. We'll get a reputation. It'll not cost us much. Your way of making money's expensive . . . creating huge debts for us. My way's using our heads and making money out of what's here.

Mary   I couldn't cope with the fuss and the people and all the coming and going.

Donald   I'm frightened we'll not be able to repay the loans.

Mary   Divven fuss about that. That's my worry.

Andy   Donald . . . if you start something like that, it's stuck there with you. And it grows and grows and it suffocates the life out of you, and the family and the beasts. We'd all suffer. All your talk of resources! Isn't the happiness of this family a resource? And our fells to walk on at will . . . without other folk . . . and ponies . . . and the mess of the campers . . . and the litter and other folks' drunkenness and the disturbance of it all? Resources isn't just for making money . . . it's for making lives better.

Donald   You're sounding like Da.

Mary   No hurt in that.

Donald   When you owe thousands for the farm and thousands for the parlour resources *is* for making money!

Andy   Not your way!

Mary   What's that?

Andy   What?

Donald   I cannot hear awt . . .

Mary   Shurrup . . .

They listen. Sound of fire in the distance. **Donald** *rushes out into the yard, then flies back into the house.*

Donald   Byre's ablaze!

Andy   You get the beasts out . . .

Donald   Mam . . . take the Landrover and seek help!

Mary   Where's the keys?

Andy   Catch!

He throws her the keys.

Donald   Howay!

They rush out.

Part Two

Spring 1980

Mary (*from her journal*)   The boys have been working themselves near to death trying to cope on the fells and keeping the milking parlour going. I wanted them to have help in, but they were both against the idea, for this year at least. They seem to have a fear that if they give one inch of their territory away, they've lost something for good. Since the fire, the milk yield has been right down, with the shock of it and the smoke getting to the cows. Andy's not been able to increase the herd as much as he should, which may be a blessing as far as the labour is concerned. But the shortage of cash, which I had bargained on from what we all thought would be extra milk sales, is playing war with the loan repayments . . .

The farm one evening. **Andy** *is servicing his fishing rod and reels.* **Mary** *is clearing away the tea things.*

Donald (*off*)   Mam . . . *Mam!*

Mary   What?

Donald (*off*)   Where's your hair dryer thingy?

Mary   What are you doing in my bedroom? Get out of there!

Donald (*off*)   Where's the hair dryer?

Mary   In the box under the bed.

Andy   Folks say Greenwell's Glory's canny. Have you still got any of those *Scottish Field* magazines, Mam?

Mary   There's a couple by the coal bucket . . . gave the rest to the jumble sale.

Andy   I never had time to read them. You might ask, like.

Mary   I pay for them.

Andy   We all pay . . . comes out of farm money.

Mary   Me that gets them in.

Andy   What's that idiot up to?

Mary   Just getting himself tidy.

Donald *comes in. He's bathed and done his hair. A clean shirt is hanging out and he's trying to get cufflinks in unsuccessfully.*

Donald   Could you do these, Mam?

Andy   Poufffff . . . what is that smell? Ughhhhh!

Donald   I found some Brut up there.

Mary   That's years old that!

Andy   Father's!

Donald   Smells canny to me. Better than smelling like a rancid udder.

Andy   Where did you get them from?

Mary   These were your father's cufflinks.

Andy   Let's see.

Mary   They were a wedding present from your Uncle Joseph. They're silver, mind.

Andy   Who said you could wear them?

Donald   No point in just leaving them in the drawer for ever.

Andy   You should still ask.

Donald   Mam doesn't mind. Mam gave them to me.

Andy   Oh?

Mary   Now . . . there's something for you too.

Andy Like what?

Mary I thought you could try his engagement ring.

Andy Can't you just leave his things together, without interfering? It's ower early to start splitting things up, like.

Mary Three years is long enough. It's best to make use of things.

Andy I'm the oldest. You should have asked me first.

Donald What's special about being the oldest, like?

Andy You should have asked us.

Mary I should have asked you together.

Andy Aye . . . that would have been better, like.

Mary I'm sorry, now. I was wrong. Howay and get dressed, Donald.

Donald leaves.

Mary I never realised you'd care so much.

Andy I do care. I still have the feeling that Da will come walking through the door. When I hear the tractor pull into the yard, I expect to hear him come banging his way in.

Mary You need to start going out more . . . like you used to. With a bit more sense, maybes . . . but you've gone too far in the other extreme.

Andy Don't start on us.

Mary You've been working ower hard. You need company . . . other folk. I'm getting away more than you now.

Andy Don't go on.

Donald comes back in.

Donald Where's the shoe polish?

Andy What a little tart you are. Why won't you tell us where you're going?

Donald 'Cos I didn't want you onto us all day long.

Andy   Where are you going, then?

Donald   Edinburgh.

Andy   For the night?

Donald   Not the whole night . . . I'll be back late on.

Andy   Edinburgh! How?

Donald   He's picking us up.

Andy   Who?

Donald   James.

Mary   James?

Donald   There's an evening of rugby films.

Andy   I thought you were sick of rugby.

Donald   Sick of Tweed, more like. How does that look, Mam?

Mary   Very good.

Andy   You don't look like my brother at all.

Donald   I don't want to look like a walking haystack . . . not in Edinburgh. Doesn't matter in Kelso . . . but they might think you're daft in Edinburgh.

Andy   They might still.

Mary   I wish someone was coming to take me out for the evening.

Donald   Have you ever thought of getting another husband, Mam?

Andy   Howay! Divven put ideas in her head, man Donald!

Donald   She's not entirely past it yet, are you Mam?

Andy   Shurrup!

Donald   You should know about that, like.

Mary   That's enough!

Andy   Stupid little bugger!

Andy *attacks* **Donald**, *wrenching his shirt and messing up his hair.*
Donald *swings at* **Andy**, *who parries the punch.*

Donald   You're mad!

Andy   Bastard!

Donald   You've snapped Da's cufflink! Look what you've done! It's broken, man! Look!

Andy *rushes from the room in distress.*

Mary   Don't be hard on him, son.

Donald   What am I going to do?

Mary   Come here. Let's have a look now. I'll have that mended in a moment.

She fetches her sewing basket and sets to work sewing the link together.

This'll do for now. We'll get it mended properly later.

Donald *is almost in tears, but doesn't want his mother to see.*

James (*off*)   Hello!

James *enters.*

James   Hello Mary . . . excuse me barging in.

Donald   Not quite ready, James.

James   Right.

Mary   That's fettled it. Now off you go and get your jacket.

Donald *goes.*

Mary   This has caught us all on the hop.

James   Sorry about that.

Mary   Donald sprung this expedition on us. Are you going to be late?

James   Not if we hurry.

Mary   I meant coming back.

James   Oh ... ha ... I thought we'd stop and have fish and chips in Dalkeith. Very important, fish and chips in Dalkeith. We'll be back before midnight.

Mary   Only he's got an early start in the morning.

James   Yes ...

Mary   His turn with the cows ... getting them started at least.

James   Right.

Donald *returns.*

Donald   I'm ready. Bye, Mam.

James   Goodbye.

They go.

Mary   Behave now!

Donald (*off*)   Try to!

When **James**'s *car has left the yard,* **Andy** *comes back into the living-room. He says nothing. He returns to his fishing gear.*

Mary   ... Mind ... there's something about fishing in *Horse and Hound*.

Andy   Where is't?

Mary   In my bedroom.

Andy   I'll seek it later.

Mary   Still early.

Andy   Beasts can look after themselves tonight ... I've finished work.

Mary   I've a proposition to make to you.

Andy   What?

Mary   Let's drive down to Allendale for the evening.

Andy   Allendale!

Mary   Aye ... you drive down ... we'll have a drink or two ... see our friends ...

Andy   ... takes an hour and a half ...

Mary   That just about gives us time.

Andy   Give us an hour maybes ... by the time you're ready to set out.

Mary   Canny chance of drinking after hours!

Andy   What's come over you, Mam?

Mary   I'll drive back, mind ... no arguments about that! *And* you come when I tell you! Do you promise?

Andy   Aye ...

Mary   ... and no stopping over the night!

Andy   No.

Mary   Well get yourself ready, lad. I'm not going out with the local scruff. Get washed and shaved ... and there's a clean shirt in the drawer.

Andy *runs upstairs to get ready*.

Mary   ... and I'll be ready to leave in ten minutes.

Duff, *dressed as the grey minstrel, entertaining the ladies of another Women's Rural Institute meeting*.

Duff   ... and Lord Belister held a great banquet on New Year's Eve and his servants were sent out far and wide to gather food and fuel. And singers, dancers and acrobats were engaged to entertain the guests. Then ... when the feast was at its height ... the Grey Minstrel entered ... and the lord commanded him to sing. And he sang the songs of the great Borders families, and the great cattle raids, and the heroic deeds of generations. And the guests were bound in a spell by the stranger.

But the other artists were jealous and they spread rumours that the Grey Ministrel was a spy sent by Lord Belister's enemies to observe the strength of the castle. And before dawn, the Grey Minstrel vanished from the castle and Lord Belister set the hounds loose in the misty darkness. And the whole company waited on the castle walls, listening to the baying hounds. And they heard the death screams of the Grey Ministrel as the hounds tore his body. At dawn they found his bloody remains.

But the Grey Ministrel's ghost still haunts the grounds of Belister. And when his song is heard through the mists, or his grey form is seen, whoever then is Lord at Belister is sure to die violently!

James *and* **Donald** *with fish and chips in Dalkeith.*

James   C . . .

Donald   E . . .

James   N . . .

Donald   T continued.

James   . . . oh . . . CENT . . . R . . .

Donald   . . . A . . .

James   . . . have you got me . . . hold on . . . ha . . . L . . . CONTINUED! L continued . . . God.

Donald   L . . .

James   Oh heck! . . . Oh heck!

Donald   You've had it, man!

James   Ohhhh what about CENTRALLIFICATION?

Donald   No such word.

James   Ohhhhh Y . . . I suppose . . .

Donald   That makes you a DOPE!

James   I'm not a DOPE am I?

Donald   You were a DOP to my DO . . . you lost the last'un . . . so that's your E . . . sorry James . . . you're a DOPE!

James   I am rather sometimes.

Donald   You are tonight, like . . . no offence, mind.

James What's your fish like?

Donald Canny.

James The whole world should know . . . that fish and chips in Dalkeith *can* be fun!

Donald Your turn to start.

James P . . .

Donald R . . .

James . . . I . . .

Donald The great thing about tonight is that we've talked about nothing serious. What is it? PRI . . . oh aye.

James OI? Challenge!

Donald No man . . . PRI . . . C . . .

James Oh Donald . . . what are you thinking of?

Donald Nothing much.

James No doubt . . . K continued . . .

Donald PRICK continued . . . what more is there? . . . er . . . L . . .

James Oh *no*! Ohhhhh . . . do you spell PRICKLY with an -EY?

Donald Nope!

James Can you be PRICKLED?

Donald Improbable, I should say.

James Oh you can PRICKLE someone. I PRICKLE; you PRICKLE; he she or it PRICKLES . . .

Donald Only if you were a horny blackberry.

James Look . . . this evening I've been a CLOT, a TWIT, a FOOL and, that ultimate humiliation, a DOPE . . . please, this once, let me PRICKLE . . .

Donald Gan on then . . . but don't start with a P again . . .

James Oh hell! Where can you pee in Dalkeith?

Donald   Not again.

James   I'm full.

Donald   There's dustbins down that alley . . . doubt if
they're big enough, mind . . .

James   Whistle properly this time . . . remember the Great
Flood of Kelso . . .

Donald   I'm coming too . . . gan on, man . . .

They disappear up the alley.

Later that spring

On the fell top. **Andy** *has been drawing drainage plans.*

Andy (*shouting*)   Donald!

Donald (*way off*)   Hello . . .

Andy   How far is't from here to the gully?

Donald (*off*)   Which gully?

Andy   Far'un . . .

Donald (*off*)   150 . . .

Andy *makes a note. He starts making all sorts of calculations about the
drainage, then packs it in. He gets out his food and pours himself a coffee
from the flask. Eventually,* **Donald** *arrives.*

Donald   Thanks for waiting.

Andy   Still hot, like. Do you want yours now?

Donald   Aye . . . gan on . . .

Andy *pours him some coffee.*

Andy   Canny few ditches needed . . .

Donald   Is it worth draining?

Andy   Huge grant, man . . . mustn't miss our chance . . .
may not last . . .

Donald Young Farmers is doing a play for the competition.

Andy Oh aye.

Donald Thought I might take a look in.

Andy Aye.

Donald Fancy it?

Andy Maybes.

Donald I wonder if there's bodies in yonder moss.

Andy Bodies?

Donald Aye . . . it preserves them. They never rot. It's the peat. They found this gadgy once . . . with a rope around his neck. He'd been dead for hundreds of years. All black he was. I saw his photograph . . . black as leather. And all the wrinkles on his face and his hair and whiskers were plain to be seen. Divven take all the sarnies . . . eh! You've had all the tomato ones!

Andy Cheese'uns there.

Donald You must have started early on the bait.

Andy Need to with you around.

Donald If we drain the fell o'er there . . . and the moss dries out . . . who knows what we may find?

Andy Cake's canny.

Donald How many drainage thingies do we need?

Andy *Tiles*, man.

Donald Drainage *tiles*.

Andy Thousands . . . hold on . . . where's some paper?

Donald I got none.

Andy *finds some paper in one of his pockets.*

Andy This'll do . . . eh . . . look at this!

Donald What is't?

Andy My poem! Remember our poems . . . last winter?

Donald Hold on now . . . mine was . . .

Andy Hey laddddd . . .

Donald Shurrup man . . . listen . . .

> When I'm mixin' Nelly's feed
> I think on buns and cake and breed
> But when at neet ah stuff ma belly
> Oot o'ma heed gans poor old Nelly.

. . . something like that . . .

Andy Is that poetry, like?

Donald 'Corse it is . . . what's yours then?

Andy Ohh no . . .

Donald Gan on . . .

Andy

> The sigh of the wind
> The bleat of the sheep
> The curlew's complaining
> The deer that do leap
> The sky larks a-chattering
> The gentle harebells
> All are a-singing
> The song of the fells.
> The frost in the winter
> The drifting of snow
> Logs for the fire
> A warm place to go
> Tractor in mornings
> With hay for the sheep
> Songs in the evening
> And early to sleep.

Donald Not exactly early to sleep with you bouncing around all night.

Andy What do you mean me?

Donald Good poem, though . . . I like the drifting snow and logs for the fire.

Andy Have you finished stuffing your face?

Donald Aye.

Andy Now . . . we need to pace out from yon dyke end to the far ditch.

Donald Hold on . . .

Andy What do you mean?

Donald We'll have a race to the dyke.

Andy Which part of the dyke?

Donald Where the gate used to be.

Andy All right . . . go!

Donald Come back here! None of your cheating. Now get in a line.

Andy, *mischievously, stands behind* **Donald** *with his pelvis thrust into* **Donald**'s *arse.*

Donald Not that sort of line! Now stay by that bit of grass.

Andy I'm ready.

Donald To your marks.

Andy Get back . . . gan on . . . six inches!

Donald To your marks . . . get set . . .

Andy . . . howay . . .

Donald *Go!*

Donald *races off with* **Andy** *in hot pursuit.*

Andy (*off*) Come back . . . *cheat!*

James *is talking to* **Mary** *at the farmhouse. They have spent hours going through the accounts and are now waiting for the boys to come home.*

James My parents were in India, you see. I went there a few times, but mostly I spent my holidays with an aunt in Tunbridge Wells. When I was seven I decided to take matters into my own hands. I knew there was an orphanage run by nuns at the other end of town. And I'd read all these books in which parentless children had the most marvellous adventures. I was especially fond of one in which the parents were killed by Red Indians and the little boy was taken away alive to be brought up like an Indian brave. Anyway . . . this summer afternoon Aunt Sylvie was busy watering the garden so I took off all my clothes and walked naked through the streets of Tunbridge Wells and strode up to the front door of the orphanage and reached up to the great iron knocker. And this old nun opened the door . . . and she stared at me in astonishment . . . and I said, 'My mother and father are dead . . . take me in!' And she screamed out and I thought, My God she sounds just like Aunt Sylvie . . . and before I knew what was happening I was whisked into this room, surrounded by a whole flock of nuns, wrapped in a blanket and perched on a table. And as I looked around at them I realised that I'd made the most ghastly error. I had swopped an old aunt, who I was experienced at making a fool of, for a whole gang of aunts . . . and there wasn't a dirty or free child in sight . . . and not a hint of adventure. So I came clean and told them where I lived. And I was taken at reckless speed through the streets in the back seat of a great black car . . . with half a dozen nuns on top of me. Aunt Sylvie was hysterical when we arrived. Police were everywhere. And I suddenly felt naked for the first time that day. Aunt Sylvie punished me by forbidding me to have a bath that night . . . which was marvellous . . . ha . . .

Mary   Donald has told me how much you enjoy bathing in the plunge with the other lads after training . . . It sounds like a sheep dip . . .

James   Yes . . . and the water is deliciously muddy . . .

The boys arrive back.

Mary   They're in.

James   Good.

Mary   I'll get some tea going.

She goes off to the kitchen. **Andy** *enters. He is very scruffy, after a day's work on the fells.*

Andy   Oh ... hello ...

James   Hello.

Andy *collapses on the sofa.*

James   Where's Donald?

Andy   Puttin' dogs away.

James   Busy day?

Andy   Aye.

James   What's the fencing like out-by?

Andy   Canny ... mostly ... dykes down in places like ... been stone-walling a canny few times ... drainin' at the minute like. I'm knackered me.

Donald *enters.*

Donald   Mam's making some tea ... hi.

James   Hi.

Donald   Better wash my hands.

James   No.

Donald   What?

James   No need ... I mean ... no need to wash them just because I'm here.

Andy   Spends all day washing hisself.

Donald   Do I nick!

Donald *leaves as* **Mary** *enters with tea.*

Mary   There you are now.

Andy   Thanks, Mam ...

Mary   Andy generally sleeps for an hour when he comes in from the fell top.

Andy   Divven tell him all our secrets.

Mary   There's yours now.

James   Thank you.

Andy   Drainage tiles is going to cost a bit, mind. Canny few needed. Got to do it, like . . . if we're going to take on more sheep . . . got to . . . going to be a job getting the JCB up there an' all . . . heck of a lot of work, like.

Donald *returns.*

Mary   Now that we're all together . . .

Andy   Ha'd on . . . what's this then?

Donald   Shut up.

Mary   This is serious now.

Andy   Gan on then.

Mary   James and me . . . we've been going over all the accounts . . . all afternoon.

Andy   Oh aye.

Donald   Shurrup man!

Mary   It's time to face up to the facts of life. Do you want to hear it from James or me?

Donald   Let James tell us.

Andy   Aye.

James   Oh . . . well . . . ha . . . bad news, I'm afraid . . . not disastrous.

Andy   Get on with it man James!

James   You've been unlucky. Right! There isn't enough cash to pay off the interest on the various loans that you have outstanding. Even though the interest rates are fixed and highly advantageous. It's really the fire that's caught you out.

Andy   Milk yield's been poor. I know that.

James   Not just poor, Andy. You're not getting enough cash back from your milk sales to keep yourselves afloat. And . . . just wait a moment . . . and . . . you've made a tactical

error in not accepting the insurance offer made to you over
the damage to the byre.

Andy   How's that, like?

James   You seem to have got it into your heads that the
byre was worth what it might have become if you'd been able
to develop it to extend the milking parlour. It only becomes
an asset on that sort of level after the work has been carried
out. At the time of burning it was just a byre and has to be
valued as such.

Andy   After tup sales we'll have money.

James   You can't wait that long. Anyway . . . by then the
debts will have grown fantastically. When things start to
slide . . . they just get out of control so fast with such large
loans involved.

Donald   What are we going to do?

Andy   We're not selling up. Never!

James   I'll tell you what you've got to do.

Mary   Tell us.

James   One . . . settle the insurance claim straight away.
Accept what the loss adjusters have offered. If you agree to
that, I'll phone through to the company and get them to send
you a cheque by return.

Andy   Ha'd on! What if we hold out a bit longer . . . till the
tup sales?

James   To put it simply . . . the receivers are going to move
in on you . . . *soon*. If you want to hang on to your farm, you've
got to take my advice.

Mary   Carry on.

James   Secondly . . . this is going to hurt . . . are you ready?

Andy   Aye.

James   You've got to slaughter the whole of the dairy herd
and take the Common Market golden handshake. You'll
make a lot of money that way. Far more than the value of the

cattle. Then you sell the milking parlour equipment. It's almost new and you should get a reasonable price. If you do all that you'll eliminate one loan altogether, you'll pay off all your outstanding interest payments . . . and . . . ha . . . you'll even have some extra cash in the bank . . .

Andy   We'll think on't!

James   All the figures . . . and letters . . . are over there. Your mother has been through the whole lot with me and will explain anything you don't understand.

Andy   We'll think on't.

James   You must act fast. I mean this week!

Andy   Hell man!

James   Bluntly . . . you're not bloody tenants any more! You're bloody landowners! And you've got to behave as such!

Donald *rushes from the room.*

Andy   Right! That's enough! You've said your bit! That's enough!

James   Yes . . . I've said my bit.

Mary   Now . . . I've got food to prepare.

Andy   I'm starving, Mam.

Mary   Of course you are. They've worked damned hard, James.

She goes to the kitchen.

James   I know. It's a good farm. You've just got to get things right.

Andy   Aye.

Donald *returns. He has a hastily wrapped package.*

Andy   Are you OK?

Donald   Aye . . . I reckon.

Andy   That's good now.

Donald   I've got James a present. There you are.

James   No need.

Andy   What is't?

Donald   Take it . . . please.

James   Thank you.

Donald   Open it.

James *opens the package.*

James   Oh.

Andy   Da's cufflinks!

Donald   Aye.

Andy   You shouldn't! They're not yours to give!

Donald   They are mine! Mam said they were! They've been mended . . . after *you* broke them!

James   That's very kind, Donald. I think these should stay in the family.

Mary *enters.*

Andy   He's given away Da's cufflinks!

James   No.

Donald   Take them . . . please.

Andy   They're not yours to give.

Donald   They are!

Mary   I think that's very generous.

James   I can't accept them.

Donald   Why not? Why not?

James   Here . . . please.

Donald   They're yours now!

Donald *runs from the room again.*

Andy   I'll gan after him.

He goes to look for **Donald**.

James   I'm terribly sorry.

Mary   It's not your problem. None of this is your problem.

James   Do you mind if I don't stay for tea?

Mary   You're very welcome.

James   I've got to see people in Keilder about some trees.

Mary   Stay a while.

James   I'm going.

Mary   Come back tomorrow ... or the next day ... please.

James   They want me to get through a pile of work by the end of the week, Mary. There's just a chance of a partnership if I play my cards right.

Mary   My family needs you. I need you. Please come back ... soon.

James   I'll try. You can always get Donald to phone my Ponteland flat in the evenings.

Mary   Stay for something to eat.

James   I'm going.

Mary   Take these.

She gives him the cufflinks. He leaves.

A week later.

Duff *is training his colts from the touchline under floodlights.*

Duff (*shouting*)   Out to Willie ... out ... *out* ... catch the bloody thing. McAndrew ... what were you doing last night? Good Jemmy ... *good boy* ... fall ... fall ... *fall* ... *yesssssss!* Heel ... *heel* ... now out ... *out* ... *ohhhhhhhhh deeeaaaaarrrrrr* ... Right ... hold it ... *hold it*, ref! OK lads ... now I want to make a couple of changes. Puffin ... you go stand off ... aye ... swap with Stoney ... aye ... that's right, lad ... and Mawson ... Donald man! Wake up, son ... you go out on the wing ... you'll do less damage there ... Monkey, you go centre ... aye ... where Mawson was ... now we'll have five

minutes hard play . . . then we'll call it a day . . . Right-oh
ref . . .

Mary (*from her journal*)   We signed all the necessary papers
today. Andy sat up half the night going through all the loan
agreements and bank statements and letters. He looked like a
condemned man the next morning, but had made his mind up
for what was best. The day they led the beasts to slaughter,
Andy lay on the sofa and wouldn't speak to anyone. The
ladies are having a fancy dress party next month . . .

Duff *on the touchline.*

Duff   *Come here, Mawson!* Aye . . . *you*, son . . . *run*, you young
bugger!

Donald *comes off the field, covered in mud.*

Duff   Oh my God . . . what am I going to do with you? *Eh?*
Eh? Tell me what's to be done. You're playing like a beginner,
Mawson. What's happened to all the promise of the start of
the season? You may think this is one of my famous jokes, but
you actually looked like a rugby player last autumn. Is it my
fault? *Eh?* Have I rubbed you up the wrong way? Are you at
war with me? Is that it?

Donald   You're picking on us.

Duff   Picking on you? Why should I do that? 'Cos you're
English? Is that what you're thinking?

Donald   You said it.

Duff   I've coached the others since they were bairns.
They've all had a bollocking from me many a time. You're
sulking! You're letting down your team mates. Did you do
this at Hadrian? Eh? Eh lad? Are you the sort that lets your
mates down!

Donald   No.

Duff   I've a mind to put you in the reserves on Saturday. I
actually thought there was a place for you in our sevens side.

Aye ... I was thinking of playing you at Hawick. You'd like that. Eh? Would you? Would you?

Donald Aye.

Duff Tell you what I'm going to do. I'm playing you in the senior colts on Saturday up at Gala if you promise to give me all you've got for a change. Is that a deal? Is it?

Donald I'll try.

Duff Promise?

Donald Aye ... am I on the wing or what?

Duff No ... outside centre ... now then ... no birds ... no booze ... no dirty books ... now get in that bath ... run ... *run!* I'm after you!

Duff *chases after* **Donald**.

James *is on the phone to* **Mary**, *who has called him from a call box.*

James I can't come tonight ...

Mary Can you not ...?

James I've been travelling all day ... out by Nenthead ... through to St John's Chapel ... I don't want to start heading north ... it's all ... ha ... too exhausting ...

Mary The boys would love to see you ...

James I'm in the bath ... or rather ... out of it ... and I've just piled a load of clothes that need washing ...

Mary Into the bath water?

James Well ... the water wasn't *that* dirty ... that's the way I always wash my things ... think of the energy I'm saving ... I've got to do it tonight. I think you've been making all the right decisions lately, by the way ...

Mary Can you make it by the end of the month ... to check things over for us?

James Of course ...

Mary Promise?

James Well ... good heavens ... I'll do my best ...

Mary Will you get a message through ... when you're coming?

James I'll try ... I'll get in touch with Donald at Tweed on training night ... OK?

Mary Thank you ...

James Look ... I've got to go now ... I've got reports to write for tomorrow ... my lords and ... ha ... masters expect me to work for a living ... for them I mean ...

Mary Right ...

James 'Bye ...

He hangs up.

Mary Goodbye ...

She puts down the receiver.

Andy *has been visiting* **Mrs Duff** *but is confronted by* **John Duff** *as he leaves the house.*

Duff Come here you!

Andy *tries to make a run for it, but* **Duff** *is too fast and brings him down with a rugby tackle.*

Duff Where are you going, son?

Andy Piss off!

Duff Do you want your fucking head pushed through that wall? Do you? Eh?

Andy Ahhhhh ...

Duff Shut it! I've been looking forward to catching you on the job. It's you that's been drinking all my beer and eating all my crisps ... eh? All the junk I've been carrying out for her! You're just a bloody kid, aren't you, son? I thought maybe she had something going with the postman or the gamekeeper ...

but it's just kids she's been going with. And what's your name, son? Eh?

Andy   Andy . . . ahhhh . . . let go of us . . .

Duff   Andy what?

Andy   Mawson . . .

Duff   Brother of Donald Mawson?

Andy   Aye . . .

Duff *lets him go.*

Duff   Shit! Shit! Shit!

Andy   What's the matter?

Duff   You fucking Mawsons are everywhere! Buggering up my colts! Screwing up my home! Will you get off my back! Get back south of the border, you fucking English cunts! If I catch you within 100 yards of my house again, Andy Mawson, I'll break your fucking legs!

Andy   I used to play rugby . . .

Duff   I don't care if you were captain of the fucking Lions! Just get out of my life!

Andy (*from a safe distance*)   Good night Fluff!

He runs. **Duff** *chases him off.*

At the farm, **Mary** *is just finishing work on* **Donald**'s *sheep costume for the Young Farmers' play.* **Donald** *is in his underpants.*

Donald   Have you finished, Mam?

Mary   Nearly. Where's Andy?

Donald   Still bathing.

Mary   Do you know your lines, now?

Donald   Aye . . .

Mary   Try this . . .

Donald *gets into his sheep outfit.*

Donald Baaaaa . . . baaaaaaaaaaaa . . . aye, it's canny!

Andy *enters. He's just been washing his hair.*

Andy Ha'd on . . . I'll just fetch out the dogs . . .

Mary Get your costume on . . . I want to see the pair of you . . .

Andy *goes off to get into his costume.*

Mary What time have you got to be there?

Donald Seven-thirty . . . it's the last but one rehearsal, this, you know.

Mary Hang on a minute . . .

She adjusts the costume.

That's more like it, now . . .

Andy *enters in his Stinkhorn the Bull outfit.*

Andy (*singing*)
I don't need a pig or a foal
I don't need a hedgehog or a mole
I don't need a chicken or a sow
All I want is a smelly old cow . . .

It's the shudder of her udder
And the tickle of her hide
It's the blaring of her moo
That gets me inside
So prick up my ears
And up onto my toes
Any old cow
And away I goes . . .

Donald He's a right show-off him, you know . . . he's called Stinkhorn . . .

Mary I'm not surprised . . .

Andy Watch out now or I'll toss you into the yard!

Donald Tossing's all he's good at!

Mary Let's hear your song now . . .

Donald   Oh Mammmmm...

Andy   He sounds like a Blackie...

Donald   Shurrup! I'm a Swaledale...

Andy   Aye... a Swaledale yow!

Donald   Not my fault I'm a yow...

Mary   Howay!

Donald (*singing*)
Farewell to all our friends every market day
Farwell to sheep and hens
All going away away
Food for the family
Roast beef and pork
Oh what ways to end our days
On the end of a knife and fork...

Andy *and* **Donald** (*singing and dancing their rehearsal steps together*)
Don't let the knackers get you down, friends
Let's all be happy for tonight
We'll sing a rousing chorus
With market day before us
And we *don't* give a damn what the farmer does
They can send our children to the butchers
We don't mind our bollocks cut away
They can fatten us and kill us
Roast us and grill us
But we'll dance shout and sing
HIP HIP HOORAY!

Mary   Who wrote all that stuff?

Donald   Duff the Fluff.

Mary   Do you want to know a secret?

Donald   Aye.

Andy   Gan on.

Mary   Don't tell anyone, mind.

Donald 'Corse not.

Mary He's been writing to me.

Andy Duff?

Donald What about?

Andy I don't want to know.

Mary Things.

Donald What things?

Mary Oh . . . this and that.

Donald About rugby?

Mary Not really. He stops us in the street. He even wanted to carry my shopping.

Donald What does he say in his letters?

Andy Divven ask.

Mary He wants to take us out!

Andy Is that it?

Donald Never!

Mary He wants to meet us and that!

Donald He's got a wife, Mam. Ask Andy!

Andy That's all finished with.

Donald What do you say, Mam?

Andy Do you want us to fill him in, like?

Donald Aye . . . we'll see him off!

Mary No . . . I've sorted it out . . . it's no problem.

Andy Why tell us?

Donald Let her.

Mary No one else, is there.

Andy Sorry.

Mary   I just don't want you to think your Mam's past it. I could still have another bairn, you know.

Donald   You're not going to are you, Mam?

Mary   I said I could ... I'm not going to, like.

Andy   There's still life in the old cow yet.

Mary   Shurrup, Stinkhorn!

Donald   James has invited me to the Hadrian fancy dress party.

Andy   Oh aye.

Donald   Shall I go like this, Mam?

Mary   Aye ... you look canny. You best get along now.

Andy   Aye.

Mary   Mr Duff says he's interested in the Landrover ... if the price is right, mind.

Andy   I'll sort it.

They exit.

Mary (*from her journal*)   The boys did well with the Young Farmers. They didn't win, but we all had a great laugh. There were folks from all over there, and we've made a lot of new friends. Donald is wearing his sheep costume to Hadrian's fancy dress disco ...

After the Hadrian fancy dress ball, **James**, *dressed as the Emperor Hadrian, and* **Donald**, *in his sheep outfit, are eating fish and chips on the way home to* **Donald**'*s farm.*

James   Damn ... too much salt.

Donald   This vinegar's full of water.

James   Those blasted disco-whatsits are too ... ha ... loud.

Donald   Can I not stay the night at Ponteland? With you, like?

James   No!

Donald   Save a long journey.

James   You've got to start work early.

Donald   No cows any more.

James   You've got to get back tonight.

Donald   You've got the morning off tomorrow. You told us.

James   I'm not taking a boy back to my place for the night. OK?

Donald   Don't call me a boy! I'm old enough to get my head shot off in Northern Ireland. OK?

James   I'm taking you home.

Donald   I want to spend the night with you.

James   No!

Donald   Is that all you can say? Do you not want to, like?

James   This conversation never happened. Right?

Donald   Of course it happened.

James   Let's get back to the car.

Donald   I don't want to get in.

James   Don't be difficult, Donald.

Donald   You don't want to understand anything, do you!

James   Are you ready?

Donald   Aye . . . take us home! Thanks for the chips, anyway!

James   I can't do any more . . .

Duff *and* **Andy** *have met up in a local bar. They've had a few drinks.*

Duff   So that just about concludes the evening's business, Andy.

Andy   Aye. It's a fair price.

Duff Aye. Now . . . I've got another proposition to put to you.

Andy Aye.

Duff Next season I'm looking for people to take an interest in the lads who're just starting out. They need an older person to give them a bit of encouragement on training nights and help with the fixtures.

Andy I've forgotten about the game, man John.

Duff You used to play. I know that. I've checked you out. James from Hadrian says you were a promising youngster.

Andy Did he say that, like?

Duff Aye. Now when the new season starts, come down. You'll know a lot of the senior colts from the Young Farmers. You can train with them for a couple of sessions. Then you take on the wee laddies, I'll give you a hand. We need new blood at Tweed. There's room for you . . . if you're willing.

Andy I'll think on't.

Duff You belong to us, now . . . you Mawsons. You may be bloody English but you're bloody Scots too!

Andy Allendale seems a canny way off now, like.

Duff It's another world. You're wi'us now, laddie! You'll have the summer to think about it.

Andy Aye . . .

Duff There's time yet this season . . . to get acquainted. Take a look down at Tweed sometime . . .

Andy Maybe . . .

Duff We *need* Donald next season . . . he's been difficult. Sort him out, Andy.

Early summer 1980

Mary (*from her journal*)   Lambing has gone well, without many losses. I still have it in mind that one day I'll move back to Northumberland. Perhaps when the boys are married and no longer have the need of me the way they do now.

There seems to be something dead in my heart. I keep thinking that I ought to want another man. But just can't bring myself to it. I feel young . . .

Harry's ghost is always going to be with us. There's a lot of his things safely stored away in the attic. The boys wear his clothes quite happily now.

The boys are playing dominoes in the farmhouse.

Andy   Are you knocking?

Donald   Ha'd on . . .

Andy   You've got to, like . . .

Donald *knocks*. **Andy** *lays down another domino.*

Andy   La-la-laaaa . . .

Donald   Hell . . .

Andy   Still knocking?

Donald (*knocks*)   Gan on . . .

Andy (*laying another*)   Te-he-heeee . . .

Donald   What you got there, like?

Andy   Wait and seeeeee . . .

Donald *knocks again.* **Andy** *lays his last domino.*

Andy   Out! Three-two to me!

Mary *enters dressed as a witch for the WI fancy dress party.*

Mary   Good evening little children! He-he-heeeeeeeee . . .

Andy   Aaaahhhhhhhhhhhh . . .

Donald   You never told us the VAT man was coming!

Andy   What shall we do?

Mary   Fee-fi-fo-fum . . .

Donald   I'll stick a thistle up your bum!

Mary   Has anyone seen my broomstick?

Andy   Aye, it's away ower the fell top.

Mary   Look. I'm being serious. I must have it. Look! Come on.

Donald   I haven't touched your broomstick.

Andy   It might be in the bathroom . . . I was cleaning mud off my wellies with it.

Mary   May your wellies leak for ever!

Mary *goes to seek the broomstick.*

Andy   The Women's Rural Institute has a lot to answer for . . .

Donald   Want another game, like?

Andy   Not really.

Donald   Just because you're winning.

Andy   Don't fancy it right now.

Donald   What are you doing tonight?

Andy   Stopping in.

Donald   That's something.

Andy   Mam's away with the Datsun.

Donald   Aye.

Mary *comes in with her broomstick.*

Mary   Andy!

Donald   Oh gawd!

Mary   Pin me up round the back.

Andy   Oh aye.

Donald   Are you sure the women will recognise you instantly as being a character out of Scottish history, Mam?

Mary   Of course they will ... there's witches in *Macbeth* you know ...

Andy   Canny few gannin' the night an' all.

Mary   Mrs Forbes is going as Sir Walter Scott ... and Mrs Kingdom is Robert Bruce.

Donald   She ought to gan as the spider.

Andy   I pity anyone going for a late night stroll in Yetholm!

Mary   Now you two behave yourselves.

Andy   Divven drink ower much.

Donald   ... and divven waste ower much on the raffles!

Mary   Hocus Pocus Malus Locus ...

Donald   Help! I'm turning into a frog!

Andy   That's all you ever were.

Mary *goes.*

Donald   Let's have baths.

Andy   Divven feel like it.

Donald   I'm feeling a bit knackered, mind.

Andy   I think I have the answer.

Donald   Oh aye.

Andy *produces half a bottle of whisky.*

Donald   Where did you get that?

Andy   It was ... a sort of present.

Donald   Who from?

Andy   An admirer ...

Donald   No chance! They must be myopic!

Andy   Oooo ... long words ...

Donald   We play this word game ...

Andy (*pouring two glasses*)   Who?

Donald   James and me . . . finished with him now . . .

Andy   I thought we hadn't seen much of him lately . . . Let's drink to wor farm . . .

Donald   The farm!

They drink.

Andy   Do you reckon Mam was hot for James?

Donald   Not the sort of person you can easily get hot about . . . not in my opinion . . .

Andy   Nothing doing there?

Donald   Na!

Andy   How are you getting on with that Duff down at Tweed?

Donald   Not good . . .

Andy   Packing in down there?

Donald   Doubt it. Too old for colts next season. Plenty of other teams. Be finished with him. I spat at him actually. He was driving this new car . . . and I was walking up to the clubhouse and he comes up behind us and I never heard him and he hoots and I jumped, like . . .

Andy   Aye . . .

Donald   . . . and I kind of swung round and there was Duff sat behind the wheel of a great white Ford . . . and I just stared at him . . . a really vicious stare, like . . . like this . . . and he's got this cassette blaring away with bagpipes or some such shit . . . and I spat a great gob of hockle splat on his bonnet . . . and he went pale and I thought he was going to run us down . . . but he backed down, like . . . wouldn't speak to us all evening, like . . .

Andy (*topping up the glasses*)   Tomorrow . . . I've got a plan . . .

Donald   Oh aye . . .

Andy Down Burn Pastures . . .

Donald Aye . . .

Andy There is a case for it . . . now the beasts are away . . . no good trying to plant beets or barley crops . . . better now to look into that plan of yours . . . the camping and caravaning and all that . . .

Donald Aye . . .

Andy Makes more sense now, like. Worth looking into at least.

Donald Can't afford to waste what we've got.

Andy No promises, mind . . . but worth looking into.

Donald Have you talked to Mam?

Andy Not yet.

Donald Maybes we'll get another car . . .

Andy Have to sometime.

Donald You've been hogging the Datsun!

Andy Have I hell!

Donald Aye . . . you have . . . keepin' up with all these old wifies you're so keen on.

Andy What lies!

Donald Surprising what you hear in the bath at the club.

Andy Let's play cards.

Donald Divven want to.

Andy Play snap!

Donald No.

Andy So what are you so keen on?

Donald What do you mean?

Andy You heard!

Donald *is wondering how to admit to his brother that he is indeed gay.*

Donald   More interested in tups than yows just now like . . .

Andy   That's exactly what I meant.

Donald   Do you mind?

Andy   Not really.

Donald   That's that then.

Andy   Aye . . . it is . . . I suppose you'll be blaming me?

Donald   No.

Andy   Good . . . let's gan poaching!

Donald   Cannot poach your own pheasants!

Andy   Bloody miles to the next bugger's.

Donald   Let's take another dram.

Andy (*pouring*)   Aye.

Donald   Maybes you should sleep in your own room . . .
from now on like . . .

Andy   Right . . .

Donald   OK . . .

Andy   Canny cold . . .

Donald   Can be . . .

Andy   No need for rules . . .

Donald   Not really . . .

Andy   I'll get the gun . . .

He fetches it.

Donald   What for?

Andy (*checking and loading it*)   Got an idea . . .

Donald   What is't?

Andy   Come out in the yard.

Donald   Why?

Andy *fetches over the torch and gives it to* **Donald**.

Donald   What's the plan?

Andy   I'm going to blast the rooks. They've been ower noisy in the mornings . . .

Donald   Leave 'em be . . .

Andy   They'll all be in their nests now. A couple of blasts'll shake 'em up a bit . . . aye . . . that'll fettle them . . .

Donald   Howay man! They're just rooks man Andy . . .

Andy   They're vermin! They've got to be kept down. We're the masters of this farm. They got to sing to our tune from now on!

Andy *goes to the door.* **Donald** *is unwilling to follow.*

Andy   Howay!

He goes into the yard. **Donald** *stands at the door.*

Silence . . .

The blast of both barrels. A furious, terrified squawking of crows.

Lent

For Michael Codron

Lent was first performed at the Lyric Studio, Hammersmith, on 24 February 1983, with the following cast:

Paul Blake, *thirteen*	Jonathan Kent
Mr Maitland (**Matey**), *seventy-two*	Wensley Pithey
Mr Edwards, *sixty-three*	Dennis Edwards
Mrs Edwards, *seventy-five*	Jean Anderson
Mrs Blake, *eighty-six*	Patience Collier

Directed by Christopher Fettes
Designed by John Otto
Lighting by Dave Horn
Sound by Matt McKenzie

Part One

Gorse Park Preparatory School. Easter holidays. 1956.

Opening of the second movement of Elgar's Violin Concerto, played by Menuhin with Sir Edward Elgar conducting.

Paul (*checking and loading the school starting pistol*) Last term we set up our own telephone service between the dorms. It was Abrahams who had the idea. He brought two sets of headphones back from Assam, where his father works. That's in India! He got some very thin copper wire . . . it was just a single strand . . . and we laid it under the lino when matron wasn't about. I don't know how it works, but when you link up the headphones at each end of the wire, you can speak into them like telephones, and you can hear what's being said! It's incredible! You can warn the others when Matey's on the prowl. The first message we got was 'HODGE HAS BEEN SICK!' There's a boy called Hodge and he was sick right at the end of *Journey Into Space* . . . all over his sheets. Matron was furious. She thinks Jet Morgan is terrible. We might not be allowed to hear it next term.

A meeting between **Mrs Blake**, **Mr** *and* **Mrs Edwards** *and* **Mr Maitland** ('**Matey**').

Mr Edwards Am I right in thinking that the last time you saw the pistol was on the Sunday after the cross country?

Matey Yes, headmaster. I had it in my room on the Saturday night . . . it had been in my room for most of the week, as a matter of fact . . .

Mrs Edwards Why?

Matey I clean it each year, Mrs Edwards. You know that.

Mrs Edwards   Does that take a week?

Matey   I like to make sure that it is in perfect working order. It sets a very bad example to the boys if you pull the trigger and nothing happens.

Mrs Blake   Quite right.

Mrs Edwards   What time on the Sunday did you bring it to the study?

Matey   You may recall, headmaster, that you were handing out the pennies to the boys for the church offertory.

Mr Edwards   I don't remember you coming in then.

Matey   I think you might, headmaster . . . on reflection. You were particularly concerned with Jameson, who you suspected of queuing up twice to supplement his pocket money.

Mrs Edwards   Where did you put the pistol?

Matey   In the drawer in the stationery cupboard.

Mr Edwards   Did you lock it?

Matey   I do not recall the drawer being locked at any time in the last thirty years.

Mrs Edwards   Have you seen the pistol since?

Matey   No.

Mr Edwards   Have you heard any boy at any time mention it?

Matey   No, sir.

Mrs Blake   Mr Maitland, what do you think would be the wisest course of action?

Matey   I think we should have a thorough search of the staff common room, and perhaps Mr Edwards and myself might be given permission to make a discreet investigation of the rooms of the absent staff.

Mrs Edwards   I'll do that.

Mrs Blake   Certainly not!

Mr Edwards   Good idea, Maitland.

Mrs Edwards   The boy is at the bottom of this!

Mrs Blake   Rot!

Mrs Edwards   We really ought to question him before we go any further.

Mr Edwards   I agree.

Mrs Blake   I can do that later.

Mr Edwards   With respect, Mrs Blake, this is an urgent school matter.

Mrs Edwards   He's waiting outside.

Mrs Blake   Why?

Mrs Edwards   I told him to.

Mr Edwards   I think he should be summoned.

Mrs Edwards *goes to the door.*

Mrs Edwards   BLAKE! BLAKE?

She shuts the door again.

He's vanished!

Paul *enters.*

Paul   Did you call, Mrs Edwards?

Mrs Blake   Don't be impertinent!

Mr Edwards   Close the door, Blake.

Paul   Yes, sir.

Mr Edwards   We are making enquiries . . .

Paul   . . . yes, sir . . .

Mr Edwards   . . . about the starting pistol . . .

Paul   . . . yes . . .

Mrs Edwards   Have you stolen it?

Paul No.

Mr Edwards Don't lie to us, Blake.

Paul I'm not, sir.

Mrs Edwards You've stolen it, haven't you!

Paul I have not!

Mrs Blake That's enough! Now then Paul. Do you know anything about it?

Paul Yes.

Mr Edwards Ahhh!

Mrs Edwards I told you!

Mrs Blake One moment please! What do you know about it, Paul?

Paul It's quite safe. What's the matter?

Mr Edwards It's been stolen.

Paul No it hasn't. Honestly, sir! I borrowed it.

Mr Edwards What?

Paul I wanted to know what it sounded like indoors.

Matey Why?

Paul I wanted to shoot the old witch!

Mr Edwards Are you mad?

Paul No, sir! Only a little, sir! It's for the end of term treat, sir!

Mrs Blake What treat?

Paul The puppet show.

Mr Edwards You're not still playing with dolls, are you Blake?

Paul In my new play, the witch gets shot with golden bullets! It makes a terrifically exciting noise, sir! Listen!

Paul *whips out the starting pistol and shoots* **Mrs Edwards**.

Mrs Edwards Aaahhhhhhhhh . . .

Paul Isn't that terrific, sir!

Mrs Blake Paul!

Matey Never point guns!

Mr Edwards Stay calm everyone! Stay calm!

Paul We're going to squirt blood through the scenery so it trickles down the walls!

Mr Edwards Don't be foolish, Paul. Hand over the gun.

Paul *gives it to* **Matey**.

Mrs Blake That was very stupid of you!

Mr Edwards Stealing is a serious offence, Blake.

Paul I didn't steal it!

Mrs Blake You should have asked permission.

Paul I did!

Mr Edwards Oh?

Paul My father said I could!

Mrs Blake Don't be absurd.

Mrs Edwards He'll murder the lot of us!

Paul I wanted to use the gun in a puppet show two years ago. Daddy said I was too young. I said when can I use it? And he said when I was thirteen. Well, I am thirteen!

Mrs Blake I won't hear such nonsense!

Mrs Edwards He ought to be punished severely.

Mr Edwards I'll handle that!

Mrs Blake Please don't interfere, Edwards. This is a family matter now. Paul, your pocket money is stopped for a week! Now go away!

Paul Yes, Mrs Blake.

Paul *goes to the door.*

Mrs Blake   And come back later.

Paul   Yes, Mrs Blake.

Paul *leaves*.

Mrs Blake   Mr Maitland, have you finished repairing the library books?

Matey   Yes, Mrs Blake. I finished them yesterday.

Mrs Blake   Are there any missing?

Mrs Edwards (*to* **Mrs Blake**)   My dear, we're running out of sheets. The senior boys seem to wear through theirs in no time!

Mrs Blake   Then bring me a list of what you want.

Mrs Edwards   I could do with some help in the laundry room.

Mrs Edwards *leaves*.

Matey   Simon Todd has gone off to Cape Town with *She*. And it looks as though Laverty is in Paris with *A Hundred and One Useful Things a Boy Should Know*.

Mrs Blake   Is the cataloguing system in good order?

Matey   I think so.

Mrs Blake   Good.

Mr Edwards   I think that's all, Maitland.

Matey   Thank you, sir.

Matey *leaves*.

Mrs Blake   Is there something else you want, Edwards?

Mr Edwards   I want to discuss the new entry for the winter term. We can easily increase our numbers to a hundred and ten, Mrs Blake. It's quite possible to get twenty-four desks into RB, eighteen into 1A and there's at least room for another three in RA2.

Mrs Blake   I won't have it! And there's an end of it!

Mr Edwards It makes perfectly good educational sense, Mrs Blake. We wouldn't have to increase the staff. It would bring in a lot more cash. Public schools are much more interested in science than they used to be. We've got to provide a science course of some sort. Mr Campbell-Jones has been holding the fort on his own long enough! But his knowledge as far as science goes isn't great. Last term he was telling the boys in 2B that sodium is used under water to burn through metal. I'm sure that's wrong.

Mrs Blake A hundred boys is too many, Edwards. It's not a family. My late husband never intended to have more than fifty boys at Gorse Park. Now we're into the nineties. That's quite enough!

There's a knock at the door and **Paul** *enters.*

Mrs Blake Go away!

Paul Sorry, Mrs Blake.

Paul *leaves.*

Mrs Blake Paul!

Paul *re-enters.*

Paul Yes?

Mrs Blake I want to walk in the garden at eleven o'clock!

Paul OK.

Mrs Blake Don't say OK!

Mr Edwards I've told you boys about that!

Paul Sorry, sir. It's holidays, sir.

Mr Edwards That makes no difference, Blake.

Paul Yes, sir.

Paul *leaves.*

Mr Edwards I'm sorry to tell you that Paul is becoming a problem around the school.

Mrs Blake I don't think so.

Mr Edwards   There were occasions last term when Paul
failed to tell the truth, Mrs Blake. Some stamps went missing
from Simpson's stamp album. I had reason to believe that
Paul was responsible. I questioned him at assembly, but he
denied all knowledge of the theft.

Mrs Blake   You were quite wrong to try and make an
example of him.

Mr Edwards   I will not make exceptions.

Mrs Blake   I'm watching you very carefully. I've known
you too long and seen too much. I know what you want.
Planning . . . scheming . . . you and Mrs Edwards together.
It's thirty-six years?

Mr Edwards   Thirty-eight years.

Mrs Blake   Half a life time, Edwards. My husband
interviewing you in the study. I remember it precisely. You
are not without qualities. But you have become cruel, in a
childish, boyish way. Spiteful man! Spiteful!

Mr Edwards   Mr Maitland would like to earn some
holiday pay. Could I suggest that he mends some of the desk
hinges and unblocks the inkwells?

Mrs Blake   That will be perfectly in order. Please tell him
that he should come and tell me how many hours he has
worked. I'll settle up with him.

Mr Edwards   Very good, Mrs Blake.

Mrs Blake   Now I'm going to walk in the garden. What's
your wife cooking for lunch?

Mr Edwards   I'm not sure.

Mrs Blake   Not that filthy macaroni cheese, I hope. I can
manage! You go first down the stairs. Is it cold? What's the
weather like? Where's Paul? PAUL! What are you doing for
the rest of the morning?

Mr Edwards   Driving to Newbury.

Mrs Blake   Again? Damn! I'm going to get my coat. Send that boy to me! PAUL!

Paul *alone, eating glucose from a packet with his finger. He is reading a book.*

Paul   This glucose belongs to Harper. If I take anything out of a tuckbox in the holidays, I always leave a note saying what I've taken. Harper liked marbles last term. He was good at it. I've left a few in his tuckbox. If he doesn't want them, we'll come to some other arrangement. It's not stealing. It's more like lending. The boys know I do it. I only go through the tuckboxes that aren't locked. Anyway, they're stupid for leaving food behind. Carter made me give him my *Dandy Annual* for half a packet of biscuits once. That was unfair on me, I thought. I quite like having the school to myself. There's quite a lot to do. There's the library. I like the gramophone and all the records. I didn't used to. But Daddy made me go to Music Club. He's dead. I'm going to play through all the records this holidays. I wish there were some boys around. Evans . . . or Price minor.

Matey *enters. He has a pile of library books.*

Matey   Your grandmother is looking for you.

Paul   Is it eleven o'clock yet?

Matey   She's sitting in the hall. What are you eating?

Paul   Glucose. Do you want some, Matey?

Matey   Is it yours?

Paul   By arrangement with Harper.

Matey   Harper . . . oh . . .

Paul   You can have some if you want, sir.

Matey   Just a dip! What's the book?

Paul   *The Prisoner of Zenda.*

Matey   Not a bad yarn.

Matey *licks his finger and sticks it into the glucose.*

Paul   Can't you persuade Mrs Blake to get a television? All the other boys seem to watch it. It's not fair. There's football matches, Matey! And plays!

Matey   It's no good, she won't budge. I'd like one in my room, but she won't allow it.

Paul   Let's smuggle one in. She won't know.

Matey   Underhand little sneak!

Paul   I'm not!

Matey   She pays my wages and looks after you. She'd be bound to see the aerial.

Paul   We could tell her it was a new lightning conductor.

Matey   She's not that daft.

Paul   I seem to be missing everything!

Matey   She's waiting for you! MOVE!

Paul *sets off to meet* **Mrs Blake**. **Matey** *goes off to the library.*

Mr Edwards, *about to set off for Newbury, is cornered by his wife.*

Mrs Edwards   You're so wretchedly weak, Bernard. Stand up to her! Good God! I'd have thought that after all these years you'd be able to cope with the silly old bitch.

Mr Edwards   Don't lose your temper, my dear.

Mrs Edwards   You're a pathetic man. She treats you like a footman.

Mr Edwards   Would you like me to change your books in Newbury, my love?

Mrs Edwards (*giving him a pile of books*)   There you are!

Mr Edwards   What would you like this time?

Mrs Edwards   Murder stories!

Mr Edwards   Very well . . .

Mrs Edwards The Blakes have had their day. She can't last for ever. The boy's mad.

Mr Edwards What's for lunch, my love?

Mrs Edwards Mince and frogspawn! Don't be late!

Paul *and* **Mrs Blake** *are walking in the garden.* **Mrs Blake** *wears a long fur coat and a broad brimmed, black straw hat.*

Mrs Blake It's really quite warm this morning.

Paul Yes.

Mrs Blake The daffodils are past their best. Are they ready to be tied down, do you think?

Paul No.

Mrs Blake The lavender's showing signs of life. I adore lavender. What did you give up for Lent?

Paul Chocolate, worse luck. What about you?

Mrs Blake Dickens. I always give up Dickens for Lent.

Paul Does that count?

Mrs Blake In my case YES.

Paul I think I'll give up Dickens for Lent next year.

Mrs Blake It's not the same for you, silly boy. We'll have a Dickens quiz! Every time you catch me out, I'll give you a penny.

Paul Good.

Mrs Blake They're all in the library. Your grandfather gave them to me when we got engaged. I presented them to the school. What have you been reading lately?

Paul *Old Saint Paul's.*

Mrs Blake Oh! Ainsworth.

Paul There's this horrible old bag . . . a bit like Mrs Edwards . . . She pretends to look after the people in the great plague. But she robs them and kills them. She dies the most horrible death, sizzling away in molten lead from the roof of Old Saint Paul's! It's really wonderful.

Mrs Blake   You were very naughty this morning.

Paul   Sorry. I've always wanted to shoot her.

Mrs Blake   You mustn't!

Paul   I want to read *The Cruel Sea*. The grown-up version. There's only the cadet version in the library.

Mrs Blake   You're not to read it! I forbid it! You're too young!

Paul   Is it that good?

Mrs Blake   It's a wicked book! Wicked! Aren't those primulas gorgeous! Oh do look at those dreadful weeds!

Paul   You know Mr Edwards gives the boys who are leaving a talk on the last morning. Privately. In his study. What does he say?

Mrs Blake   Not much.

Paul   But what does he say?

Mrs Blake   It's man's talk!

Paul   But what?

Mrs Blake   Do smell the lilac!

Paul   I know he says something important. What is it, Mrs Blake?

Mrs Blake   If you pass your Common Entrance next term, you'll find out, won't you.

Paul   Can't you tell me?

Mrs Blake   No I can't! Now shut up!

Paul   If I pass my Common Entrance, will you buy a television set?

Mrs Blake   Certainly not!

Paul   They have Dickens on television. In serials. Oh please, Mrs Blake.

Mrs Blake Your father agreed with me. It wastes too much time. There are plenty of other things to do. Your poor father . . .

Paul We watched the coronation.

Mrs Blake Coronations are different! I don't want to hear any more about it. I think Matey should set you some extra work.

Paul Oh please NO!

Mrs Blake You want to do well in your exams. Your father would have given you work to do. You must study for at least an hour a day. I insist! I'll speak to Matey at lunch time.

Paul Do I have to?

Mrs Blake We must have flowers on the table. Be an angel boy and pick a few of those daffodils . . . and something with leaves.

Paul *goes off to gather flowers.*

Mrs Blake And I'm going to sit in the hut! Bring them to me! It's stifling! Absolutely stifling! This beastly coat!

She goes to the hut.

Sir Thomas Beecham conducting 'The Arrival of the Queen of Sheba'.

Mr Maitland *is mending a desk.* **Paul** *enters with a pack of cards.*

Paul Let's play pontoon, Matey.

Matey I'm busy.

Paul Oh come on, sir.

Matey Who taught you to play that?

Paul Someone.

Matey One of the boys?

Paul Very likely.

Matey What stakes do you play for?

Paul   Fruitgums. Smarties. Whatever's available.

Matey   I haven't got any.

Paul   Let's play anyway. We can owe each other.

Matey   Do you trust me?

Paul   Of course I do! We're still allowed secrets.

Matey   Oh?

Paul   We don't have to tell each other everything, but we can still trust one another.

Matey   Right.

Paul   Good.

Matey   Who's banker?

Paul   Cut for it.

They cut.

I am. We'll play for imaginary pennies.

Matey   Right.

Paul *deals a card each, which they look at.*

Paul   Top stake of threepence.

Matey   One penny.

Paul *deals a second card each.* **Matey** *looks at his.*

Matey   Buy for two.

Paul   You can't buy for more than your original stake.

Matey   Buy for one then.

Paul *deals him a card face down.* **Matey** *looks at it.*

Matey   Stick.

Paul *turns over his own cards.*

Paul   Ummm . . . pay eighteens.

Matey   Seventeen . . . I owe you one penny.

Paul   Tuppence. You bought for one as well as your original stake.

Mr Edwards *comes in.* **Paul** *pockets the cards.*

Mr Edwards   What have you got in your pocket?

Paul   My hand, sir.

Mr Edwards   What else?

Paul   Nothing much, sir.

Mr Edwards   What is it?

Paul   Private property.

Mr Edwards   Mr Maitland?

Matey   You never know with boys, headmaster.

Mr Edwards   Really, Maitland?

Paul   May I go now, sir?

Mr Edwards   Empty out your pockets, Blake.

Paul   No, sir.

Mr Edwards   Did you hear that, Maitland? Empty them, Blake.

Paul   It's holiday time, sir. I've gone home.

Mr Edwards *grabs him, but is knocked back by* **Paul**, *who wrenches himself free.*

Paul   Never touch me again! NEVER!

Mr Edwards   Calm down! Come to my study at 12.30. Mr Maitland, there are copies of *The Coral Island* and *Dog Crusoe* behind the blackboard in 2A.

Matey   Yes sir.

Mr Edwards *leaves.*

Matey   Damn!

Paul   I agree.

Matey   Are you going?

Paul Yes. I'm going.

Matey Look . . . Paul . . . I'll talk to him.

Paul No. I'm all right. What's the time?

Matey You've got ten minutes.

Paul Will you take me to see a film this afternoon? I'll get the money off Mrs Blake.

Matey What's on?

Paul *Buffalo Bill*.

Matey Who's in it?

Paul Joel MacRae.

Matey If you can get permission.

Paul That man is absolutely bloody, Matey.

Matey I'm sorry.

Paul I'll see you at lunch. It's one of Mrs Edward's poisonous minces.

Matey I better fetch those books.

Paul You'll find five Jennings books on top of the 2A cupboard!

They leave.

Sir Thomas Beecham conducting the hornpipe from Handel's 'Water Music'.

Mrs Blake *and* **Mrs Edwards** *enter from different directions. Each is carrying a large basket full of clothes that they have been gathering up from all over the school.*

Mrs Blake My dear – that does look heavy!

Mrs Edwards I'm dying on my feet!

Mrs Blake Have you done the changing room?

Mrs Edwards Of course.

Mrs Blake   I've done the whole of West Wing . . . 3A and
3B . . .

Mrs Edwards (*fishing out clothes from her basket*)   Tench must
have left with an empty trunk.

Mrs Blake   I think matron finds Lawrence dormitory too
big to handle!

Mrs Blake *is examining a baggy pair of pants that appears to be
unmarked.*

Mrs Edwards   Whose are those?

Mrs Blake   These are the pants that dare not speak their
name!

Mrs Edwards   Good God! I think they're Bernard's!
Where did you find them?

Mrs Blake   In the art room!

Mrs Edwards   Oh they CAN'T be. My dear, he even
sleeps in his underwear!

Mrs Blake   Filthy habit!

Mrs Edwards   Filthy men!

Mrs Blake   You do the pavilion, the gym and senior
showers . . .

Mrs Edwards   I'll do the masters' bedrooms.

Mrs Blake   I hardly think you should.

Mrs Edwards   My dear, they must be checked by
someone.

Mrs Blake   Very well.

Mrs Edwards   Now if you'll bring your collection to the
laundry room after lunch, we'll sort everything out then.

Mrs Blake   Good!

Mrs Edwards   I've borrowed the Cluedo set from the
library!

Mrs Blake   I *may* provide some refreshment!

Mrs Blake *leaves*.

Mrs Edwards   . . . in the laundry room with a hatchet!

She leaves in the opposite direction.

Paul *arrives at* **Mr Edward**'s *study*.

Mr Edwards   I've been wanting to have a talk with you . . .
er . . . Paul. Have you anything particular to say to me? About
this morning, I mean?

Paul   No sir.

Mr Edwards   Do you not feel you owe me an apology?

Paul   No sir. Why, sir?

Mr Edwards   Paul, when your parents were . . . killed, do
you remember what I said to you?

Paul   I think so, sir.

Mr Edwards   What did I say?

Paul   I'm not sure, sir. I'm not sure of the exact words, sir.

Mr Edwards   I don't need the exact words. What was the
sense of what I said to you?

Paul   I was to talk to you. If I wanted to.

Mr Edwards   I said you could look upon me as a father,
didn't I? I've known you since you were born. Well, didn't I
say that to you?

Paul   You may have done, sir.

Mr Edwards   It's a simple question. Did I, or didn't I?

Paul   You may have done, sir.

Mr Edwards   Don't start on one of your obstinate moods,
Blake! I know what I said. I know what I meant. I know why I
said it!

Paul   So do I, sir.

Mr Edwards   You have become a rude and disruptive boy, Blake. Instead of setting the sort of example to the other boys that your dear father would have wanted, you have become sly, deceitful, untrustworthy, and unmanageable! A bad example! There's no doubt in my mind that you've been stealing things from the other boys. Your stubborn defence in assembly at the end of last term just made matters worse.

Paul   I don't steal things, sir.

Mr Edwards   You were defying my authority in front of the whole school. I cannot tolerate that, Blake.

Paul   I was not guilty. I'm allowed to defend myself. I'd like to go now, sir, if I may.

Mr Edwards   No, you may not go!

Paul   Sir, I am on holiday. I am at home. I am not at school!

Mr Edwards   Don't answer back!

Paul   I have one more term left. Then I'll be going away to public school.

Mr Edwards   If you pass your Common Entrance.

Paul   Yes. If I pass.

Mr Edwards   Until that happens, whether you like it or not, Blake, I'm your headmaster. I act in *loco parentis*. I will not be answered back in front of other boys, or for that matter, in front of members of staff. Isn't it quite reasonable that I should be treated with respect? Well, isn't it? Haven't you got an answer? No answer, Blake?

Paul   My father loathed you.

Mr Edwards   Is that your answer?

Paul   He would never have wanted you to be headmaster. You were senior master because you had been here so long. That's all!

Mr Edwards   Typical Blake arrogance! They'll knock hell out of you at public school. They won't stand for it, Blake. My God, you're going to suffer!

Paul I'd like to go now, sir.

Mr Edwards I'm not ready to let you go, Blake. You realise that it would be quite impossible for me to appoint you a prefect next term? Would you like to be a prefect? Answer the question, boy!

Paul That's two questions, sir.

Mr Edwards So do I take it that you are turning down the possibility of being one of my prefects? Well, don't start spreading gossip that you've been overlooked. You've turned it down, Blake. No special tea! No prefects outing! Oh well. You had your chance. But it's not important to you. You'll be sitting on the junior table for meals, of course. No special privileges for you, even if you were once the headmaster's son! It's been your choice, Blake. I'm glad that we've sorted that out.

Paul May I go now, sir?

Mr Edwards There's one final thing, Blake. You haven't been coming to Stamp Club recently. You used to be interested in stamps. Stamps are a very good education, Blake. Valuing... buying... selling. You increase your knowledge of world geography. Stamp Club members do well in the geography CE exam, Blake. Don't say you're losing interest!

Paul No.

Mr Edwards Your father started me off, actually. And your grandfather started him off. They both had fine collections. Have you seen them?

Paul Not recently.

Mr Edwards I should very much like to look through them sometime. Do you know where they are, Paul?

Paul No, sir.

Mr Edwards Where did you last see them?

Paul I'm not sure, sir.

Mr Edwards They must be kept safe, Paul. You've got to learn to look after things. You take everything for granted, living here. I know that. But you must start to take pride in things. Where do you suppose the stamp albums are?

Paul I imagine that they are being kept safe for me until I am twenty-one, like this school, Mr Edwards.

Mr Edwards That's a long way off. You've got a lot to learn before that happens.

Paul Just seven and a half years, Mr Edwards.

The gong sounds for lunch.

Mr Edwards Well, that's all, Blake. Let's see what my dear wife has cooked up for us today.

They go off to lunch.

Harry Mortimer playing the third movement of Haydn's Trumpet Concerto.

Paul *Buffalo Bill* was one of the best films I've ever seen. You saw his whole life, from when he was a boy like me, until he was practically dead. I liked it before he was famous. At the end, he had a circus, and you knew what an exciting man he had been. But the people didn't really care, and when he was old, with a white beard, he appeared in the circus ring for the last time. And he took off his hat to the crowd and the spotlights went off him one by one. And when the lights went back on again, he wasn't there, and you knew that was the end of him and he was going to die. That bit made me cry. Matey thought it was good too. He always gives me treats in the holidays.

Mrs Blake (*off*)   Paul! Paul!

Paul I bet she gives me a job to do while *The Goon Show* is on.

Paul goes off to see what **Mrs Blake** *wants.*

Matey *has collected a tray of supper from the kitchen. He is waylaid by* **Mrs Edwards**.

Mrs Edwards Stop there!

Matey   I've just helped myself, if you don't mind.

Mrs Edwards   You know perfectly well we agreed that if staff were going to be late for supper, they would let me know in advance, Mr Maitland.

Matey   I had to do some work on my car, and I didn't think you would like me coming into the kitchen in my overalls.

Mrs Edwards   I wouldn't have liked that at all.

Matey   Right-oh, then.

Mrs Edwards   I want to see what you've taken!

Matey   I'm in a hurry, if you don't mind.

Mrs Edwards   I won't detain you long. I think I'll have to take this banana. And . . . oh dear! The rule about not more than two roast potatoes still applies in the holidays, Mr Maitland.

Matey   There were plenty left, Mrs Edwards.

Mrs Edwards   Rules must be obeyed.

Matey   Good night!

Mrs Edwards   You're seeing too much of the boy.

Matey   Oh?

Mrs Edwards   Don't overdo it. Take care.

Matey   I don't need your advice on how to run my life.

Mrs Edwards   No one is indispensable, Maitland.

Matey   Good night, Mrs Edwards.

He goes off to his room.

Mrs Edwards   I haven't finished yet! Damn the man!

She goes back to her flat.

The end of the third movement of Haydn's Trumpet Concerto, with Harry Mortimer.

Paul *is with* **Mrs Blake**.

Mrs Blake   Why won't you tell me anything, you bad boy!

Paul   There's nothing much to tell you.

Mrs Blake   I can only find out what's going on if people tell me. I know you're having problems with Mr Edwards. I know quite well what he's like.

Paul   I don't want to talk about it. I don't like sneaking. Mrs Blake?

Mrs Blake   What?

Paul   I'd like to travel.

Mrs Blake   Don't be absurd! What do you mean?

Paul   I've never been anywhere yet. I'd like to go to France, Italy, Greece . . .

Mrs Blake   Filthy foreigners! Filthy habits! Filthy food!

Paul   Have you ever been abroad?

Mrs Blake   Certainly not! You're far better off where you are.

Paul   How am I ever going to know anything?

Mrs Blake   How many plants can you name in the garden?

Paul   A few.

Mrs Blake   I bet you a penny you can't name more than ten. I'll test you tomorrow morning. How many different birds do you know?

Paul   Sparrows, thrushes, blackbirds, robins, blue tits, chaffinches . . . er . . . jays . . . rooks . . . ravens . . .

Mrs Blake   What's the difference between a rook and a raven?

Paul   Ravens are twice the size. I know quite a few birds.

Mrs Blake   And beetles? Butterflies?

Paul   I'm not so good on beetles.

Mrs Blake   There's a great deal going on right under your nose that you don't know about. If you don't know anything, blame your own laziness!

Paul   Well . . . you're right, up to a point.

Mrs Blake   Of course I'm right!

Paul   But I don't know about people! Except from boys, teachers and books. I don't know about people from real life. I want to see things for myself not read about them. Would you be angry if I ran away?

Mrs Blake   Livid!

Paul   Do I have to go to a public school?

Mrs Blake   Of course!

Paul   Aren't there schools where you can train to be an actor?

Mrs Blake   Don't be absurd!

Paul   Would you send me to a school like that?

Mrs Blake   Certainly not! Your father would have had a fit!

Paul   He might have done. I'm not sure. I don't mind leaving Gorse Park. But I don't want to go somewhere even worse!

Mrs Blake   Rude, ungrateful child!

Paul   Oh . . . you know what I mean! If I find out about schools where you can be an actor, will you think about sending me there?

Mrs Blake   You don't know what you're saying! One of these days it'll be my turn to be gathered in. Until that happens, I want to see the best happen for you. I'm quite sure your father, and your dear mother, would have wanted you to pass your Common Entrance well, and to go to a good boarding school. I'm convinced of that! And that's what is going to happen! Now please accept my decision. Be an angel boy and don't make life impossible for me.

Paul Can I go now?

Mrs Blake Where to?

Paul I'm missing *The Goon Show*.

Mrs Blake A stupid programme! Stupid!

Paul I don't think so.

Mrs Blake Come back and see me later!

Paul OK!

Mrs Blake Don't say that!

Paul OK!

Paul *goes.*

Mr Edwards *is in his flat with his wife.*

Mrs Edwards He knows perfectly well that he's not to help himself. It's been going on for twenty years, and it's got to stop!

Mr Edwards Of course, my dear. I'll see to it in the morning.

Mrs Edwards And those daffodils that arrived on the lunch table. They came from our part of the garden! It's that wretched boy. You must speak to him! He'll grow up to be a teddy boy! Just you see. It's breeding. That mother of his was a junket! An absolute junket! He'll never be a gentleman. Never!

Mr Edwards Would you like to read the paper, sweetheart?

Mrs Edwards There's nothing worth reading.

Mr Edwards There's an interesting new murder on page three.

Mrs Edwards Why didn't you tell me? Ohhh ... yes ...

She reads the paper.

Mr Edwards   I've been thinking about the summer holidays.

Mrs Edwards   Shut up, Bernard!

Mr Edwards   Sorry, my dear. There was another woman in the case. That's the prime cause of all the trouble, I think you'll agree.

Mrs Edwards   You know nothing about such things!

Mr Edwards   I know. I know!

She throws the paper aside.

Mrs Edwards   It's the violence in men. They're not to be trusted. I don't even trust you. You'd love to murder me, wouldn't you!

Mr Edwards   Please don't start on that one at this time of night. I've done everything I can for you, but there are limits.

Mrs Edwards   How would you like to do it? Would you like to grab me by the throat and shake me back and forth, throttling the life out of me? Ohh . . . I can feel your flabby fingers round my neck. Or would you rather put rat poison in my nightly bovril? My heart exploding in my chest?

Mr Edwards   My dear, why not read the church magazine?

Mrs Edwards   Did you order the Good Friday fish?

Mr Edwards   Oh drat! I'll drive in and get it tomorrow.

Mrs Edwards   How dull you are!

Mr Edwards   I thought the Camargue would be wonderful this year.

Mrs Edwards   It's unhealthy. Too many mosquitoes.

Mr Edwards   Perhaps you would prefer the Canary Islands?

Mrs Edwards   Too far. Those beastly planes! I'd like to go to Scotland by train.

Mr Edwards   That's settled, then. You *shall* go to Scotland. I shall go to the Camargue!

Mrs Edwards   You'll be bitten to death! Good!

Mr Edwards   I'm going out for a walk.

He leaves.

Mrs Edwards   Bernard!

She follows him.

In **Matey**'s *room,* **Paul** *and* **Matey** *have been listening to* The Goon Show. *It is just finishing.* **Matey** *switches off the radio.*

Paul   It's been a really good day.

Matey   Not bad.

Paul   I loved the film.

Matey   Yes.

Paul   I wish Gorse Park would be attacked by Indians.

Matey   Time for a brew. Will you join me?

Paul   Yes please, sir.

Matey   You've been very quiet about your interview with the head.

Paul   He's not making me a prefect next term. I don't care really. I hope Anthony Ryecroft will still be my friend.

Matey   I'm sure he will.

Paul   I think so.

Matey   Did you dispose of the cards?

Paul   He didn't even mention them. We're allowed cards for Bridge Club. And for the Magic Circle Club. We should be allowed them all the time. Rules shouldn't count in the holidays.

Matey   Have you been doing any revision?

Paul   Not much.

Matey   It's worth doing some. CE is only weeks away now.

Paul   That's what Mr Edwards says.

Matey   He's right.

Paul   I hate him. The only time I like him is in class. He becomes a different person. Almost a performer. He's a good teacher. I hate him as a man.

Matey   Things will get better when you get away from here.

Paul   Mr Edwards hopes things will get worse! I'm not looking forward to public school. I don't know what I'm going to do. If I'm not going to be a prefect, I might as well be as bad as possible.

Matey   How?

Paul   Once the exams are over, I thought I'd sneak off to the cinema more often. I'm also doing a final puppet show for the end of term. Price minor has some good ideas. They're all secret, of course. I wish Mr Edwards wouldn't call my puppets dolls. He says, 'The boys who like playing with dolls are doing something in the Common Room after tea . . . ' That's supposed to be our announcement in assembly! As if we were girls or something.

Matey *gives* **Paul** *a cup of tea.*

Paul   Thanks, sir.

Matey   You've been listening to a lot of records lately.

Paul   I'm going through the whole collection. Some of the best ones never get played at Music Club.

Matey   What are the best ones?

Paul   You'll think this is really soppy of me, but I found a record of Gigli singing *Agnus Dei*.

Matey   What does that mean?

Paul   Lamb of God.

Matey   Good boy.

Paul It's all in Latin. I don't like it when it starts, but when he starts to sing, my hair stands right on end!

Matey What else?

Paul There's the *Arrival of the Guests* by Wagner.

Matey *V*argner.

Paul That's good. I like the trumpets. I'm thinking of using it in the puppet show. The trouble is, we've only got eleven puppets and I don't see how we can have them all marching on stage and make it last three minutes.

Matey I see what you mean.

Paul The puppets have fixed characters. So you've got to keep using the donkey, the skeleton and the witch whether you like it or not. I thought of having the skeleton singing *Agnus Dei*. Do you think the boys would like that?

Matey Yes.

Paul You could have it crawling out of the grave during the opening bit, then it could sing *Agnus Dei*, then it could crawl back into the grave! I think that would be good. I've been trying to imagine it in my mind. When you're not there any more. Mr Edwards said they died instantly. That means 'in a moment . . . in the twinkling of an eye'. They were there, then they weren't. If I'd seen it, I could understand it better. It must be like the lights switched off in the dorm. There's a time when your eyes are getting adjusted to the dark. You can't see anything. It takes time to find you still exist. What happened to you when you were young, Matey?

Matey Nothing like that.

Paul But you were in the Great War.

Matey Yes.

Paul Why didn't you ever get married?

Matey Well . . . now then . . .

Paul Sorry, sir.

Matey Let me tell you a secret.

Paul   Yes!

Matey   I was married!

Paul   Good heavens!

Matey   I got married in 1919.

Paul   Good heavens!

Matey   It only lasted two years, Paul. It didn't suit us. That's my secret. You mustn't tell Mrs Blake. She wouldn't approve.

Paul   I promise, Matey. She may still be alive! She'd be dreadfully old by now. Do you ever see her?

Matey   I haven't seen or heard a word from her since 1921!

Paul   That's the most amazing secret anyone has ever told me.

Matey   Now shut up and drink your tea!

Paul   Matey...

Matey   What?

Paul   This place will belong to me when I'm twenty-one.

Matey   Yes.

Paul   I want you to know that whatever happens, this is going to be your home. Even if you live to be a hundred, Matey. I promise you.

Matey   My dear boy...

Paul   Who is your favourite author?

Matey   Kipling.

Paul   I thought you'd say that.

Matey   Why?

Paul   Because you always read *Stalky and Co.* to the boys at the end of term. Why is Kipling so good?

Matey   You know... I'm not sure. He was *the* great writer of my boyhood. It's easier to stay loyal to boyhood heroes. I can still feel his voice at my shoulder when I read him, like a ghost. His son was killed in the war, you know.

Paul   Was he?

Matey   He did wonderful work for the War Graves Commission. He's a writer I would stand by, right or wrong.

Paul   I've read *Puck of Pook's Hill*, *The Jungle Book* and *Captains Courageous*. I thought I was going to like *Kim*, but I found it difficult. And I utterly refuse to walk around the school with a book called *Wee Willie Winkie* in my pocket, even if the stories *are* good! I think there are too many words in Kipling.

Matey   There are *far* too many words in Sir Walter Scott!

Paul   Telling me! Do you know, Henshaw actually reads Walter Scott for pleasure! He even got a hundred lines for reading *Redgauntlet* under the desk in science! I think he should have been awarded a Nobel Prize for tolerance! What's the time?

Matey   Late.

Paul   I've got to go and see Mrs Blake before bedtime.

Matey   Yes.

Paul   Thanks for the tea.

Matey   Right-oh.

Paul *leaves*.

Mrs Edwards *is visiting* **Mrs Blake**.

Mrs Edwards   And I must tell you that we need two dozen new sheets for next term. Now that's not at all bad. It's some years since we bought new sheets. And the roller towels in the upstairs washrooms and in the back lavatories . . . the latest educational thinking is that roller towels are not safe! There were two cases, in different parts of the country, last term, in which children hanged themselves with roller towels. Whether or not these were cases of suicide, or whether they were accidents . . . a boy goes to dry his hands, slips, and hangs himself by mistake . . . or whether there is some other sinister explanation . . . I cannot tell.

Mrs Blake   What do you suggest in their place?

Mrs Edwards   Paper towels!

Mrs Blake   Filthy things! Too American!

Mrs Edwards   But far safer!

Mrs Blake   The boys might eat them and choke to death!

Mrs Edwards   There will be such a saving on the laundry bills. We must do it, my dear.

Mrs Blake   Oh very well.

Mrs Edwards   Good! I knew you'd see sense eventually.

Mrs Blake   You must be tired, Frances.

Mrs Edwards   Oh no.

Mrs Blake   You must be worn out!

Mrs Edwards   Not really.

Mrs Blake   I am!

Mrs Edwards   Poor Mrs Blake. I'll bring you your beef tea.

Mrs Blake   How heavenly!

Mrs Edwards   It's nothing.

Mrs Blake   You're an absolute saint!

Paul *knocks and enters.*

Mrs Blake   Mrs Edwards is just about to be canonised!

Paul   Good!

Mrs Edwards   Have you had a nice day, Paul?

Paul   Yes.

Mrs Edwards   What a great pity about this morning. Oh well! I better be off to the kitchen.

Mrs Edwards *leaves.*

Mrs Blake   I don't want to know about this morning.

Paul   She likes trying to get me into trouble.

Mrs Blake   Now my dear, have you had enough to eat?

Paul   Yes thank you.

Mrs Blake   You do wash properly before you go to bed?

Paul   Yes.

Mrs Blake   I mean . . . properly?

Paul   Yes.

Mrs Blake   Why don't you move out of the dormitory in the holidays?

Paul   I'm used to the bed. I like having the place to myself.

Mrs Blake   You've a perfectly good room of your own.

Paul   It's no good with a bed in. There's not enough room for the puppets and the stage. I wish I'd never left the private side. I hate the way Mr Edwards has taken it over. Why didn't you take it over? You could have come to live with me there. I wouldn't have minded.

Mrs Blake   Out of the question! I must be near the dormitories.

Paul   He's taken my home from me.

Mrs Blake   You'll just have to make the best of things.

Paul   I'm trying to.

Mrs Blake   How's Mr Maitland?

Paul   All right.

Mrs Blake   He's getting dreadfully old, you know.

Paul   Would it be possible for me to have some more pocket money, Mrs Blake?

Mrs Blake   A shilling a week is *quite* enough!

Paul   It cost one-and-six to go and see a film.

Mrs Blake　Your father always thought that a shilling was plenty.

Paul　He would have given me more now.

Mrs Blake　Rot! Too much money is bad for a boy! Thoroughly bad!

Paul　Can't I do some jobs? Like Matey? I could weed the garden. I could earn some more money, Mrs Blake. I won't waste it.

Mrs Blake　You'll just spend it on sweets.

Paul　I won't. I want to see another film. I want to buy a record. I want some books.

Mrs Blake　The school has plenty of books.

Paul　Not the sort I want. I like prison-camp books. Books about the war. Escaping through enemy territory.

Mrs Blake　You're too young.

Paul　I'm not. Phillips had a book about Japanese prison camps last term. We all read it. It didn't do us any harm.

Mrs Blake　There are plenty of good books to read.

Paul　I read good books, Mrs Blake. Last term I read *A Tale of Two Cities* with Mr White. And *The War of the Worlds*. And *Crime and Punishment*.

Mrs Blake　Don't tell lies! You never read *Crime and Punishment*!

Paul　I did!

Mrs Blake　What's it about?

Paul　The man who killed people with an axe and felt very guilty about it afterwards. Actually, the version I read was the 'Classics Comic' version. It was quite boring. The murder was quite good, but nothing much else happened, as far as I could see. The proper book might be better. You can't put everything into pictures, can you . . .

Mrs Blake　Comics are bad for your eyes!

Paul   I do need more money, Mrs Blake.

Mrs Blake   Very well. We'll talk about it after Easter.

Paul   That's a week away! I want to see another film next week. I'm not allowed to see films in term time. I'll only be able to see three films between now and the summer holidays. Please let me work for pocket money?

Mrs Blake   Your father would not approve.

Paul   He would!

Mrs Blake   You can do some weeding tomorrow morning.

Paul   Thank you!

Mrs Blake   I'll pay you threepence an hour.

Paul   Thank you, Mrs Blake!

Mrs Blake   And not a penny more!

Paul   Of course not.

Mrs Blake   Now be an angel and see what's happened to my beef tea.

Paul   I don't know how you drink the stuff. I don't mind the smell of it, but it tastes horrible.

Mrs Blake   It keeps me alive. Now fly!

Paul *leaves, flapping his arms.*

Mrs Blake   And don't fall down stairs!

Paul (*off*)   OOOOOkkkkkkaaayyyyyy!

Mr Edwards *is walking round the school. He meets* **Paul** *on his way to the kitchen.*

Mr Edwards   Good evening, Paul.

Paul   Good evening, sir.

Mr Edwards   Isn't it time you were in bed?

Paul   Mrs Blake has sent me down to the kitchen, sir.

Mr Edwards   My wife will bring her Bovril along presently.

Paul   Thank you, sir.

Mr Edwards   Paul.

Paul   Yes, sir?

Mr Edwards   You haven't been in Mr Maitland's room tonight, have you?

Paul   No, sir.

Mr Edwards   You're quite sure about that?

Paul   Yes, sir.

Mr Edwards   I see.

Paul   May I go now, sir?

Mr Edwards   It's against the rules for boys to visit masters in their rooms.

Paul   Yes, sir. Why, sir?

Mr Edwards   The masters' rooms are out of bounds.

Paul   Even if the master invites you into his room, sir?

Mr Edwards   Has Mr Maitland been inviting you into his room?

Paul   No, sir.

Mr Edwards   Are you sure?

Paul   He hasn't, sir.

Mr Edwards   For boys and masters to be found together is a very serious matter.

Paul   Yes, sir. Why, sir?

Mr Edwards   Stop pestering me, Blake.

Paul   Yes, sir. But why, sir?

Mr Edwards   You'll have to wait until my school leavers' talk.

Paul   But what do you say, sir? What's your talk about?

Mr Edwards   Wait and see, Blake.

Paul   Why can't you tell me now, sir?

Mr Edwards   You are becoming quite intolerable, Blake!

Paul   Sir...

Mr Edwards   What?

Paul   There is one master I've been with.

Mr Edwards   What?

Paul   There is, sir.

Mr Edwards   What?

Paul   I've been alone with one master quite a few times, sir!

Mr Edwards   I suspected as much! Who?

Paul   I've often been alone with... *you, sir!* I have, sir! I've often been in your study. I've even visited you in what used to be my house, sir!

Mr Edwards   Don't be absurd, Blake!

Paul   I have, sir, haven't I?

Mr Edwards   Just... just... just *stop it Blake!*

Paul   But I don't understand, sir!

Mr Edwards   Go to bed!

Paul   I'm not ready to.

Mr Edwards   Do what you're told!

Mr Edwards *attacks* **Paul**.

Paul   Go away! *Go away!*

Mr Edwards   I'm not putting up with this!

Paul   Neither am I!

Mr Edwards   My God! My wife is right! You *will* end up a teddy boy!

Paul   All I want is to be left alone. In my own home. Just left alone!

Mr Edwards   You spend too much time on your own. You're going out of your mind, Blake. You're becoming a thoroughly odd child.

Paul   I'm not a child!

Mr Edwards   Good night, Blake!

Mr Edwards *leaves.*

Mrs Edwards *comes from the kitchen with* **Mrs Blake***'s cup of Bovril. She doesn't see* **Paul***.*

Paul   Good night . . .

Mrs Edwards   AAAHHHHHHHHH.

She almost drops the cup and saucer.

You wicked boy! *Wicked*!

Paul   Sorry, Mrs Edwards.

Mrs Edwards   If you ever do that again, I'll kill you!

Paul   Good night, Mrs Edwards.

She proceeds to **Mrs Blake***'s room.*

Paul   The boys would all be in bed by now. I sleep with them, rather than in my own room. The place seems so quiet without them, even at this time of night. The classrooms all have their own smell . . . ink and wood. The changing rooms smell of socks and damp mud. The back lavatories, where we play marbles, of old disinfectant and lavatory paper. If you took me into any part of the school I could tell you exactly where I was just by using my nose. On a night like this, any sound that I hear . . . the closing of a door . . . a flush of water . . . tells me who is where, and what they are doing. I know this whole place. It's where I've spent my entire life. I've been to London three times, but not since my parents died. Since then, I've only been to Newbury, and to some of the nearby schools to play football and cricket. In term time, the *Daily Telegraph* is put into the library each day. Mr

Edwards gives us lectures about not just reading the sports pages. There's no paper at all in the holidays. Mrs Blake never has one. I try to listen to the news on the radio.

There's a sound on the stair.

I can hear Matey coming down to raid the kitchen. He's been doing this since before I was born!

Matey *comes in. He is in his dressing-gown and slippers, and is carrying his tray back to the kitchen.*

Paul   Matey... don't be frightened.

Matey   Good Lord!

Paul   I feel like staying up all night.

Matey   Are you all right?

Paul   Yes. I like it when I can get this place to myself. I'm not really going to stay up. I'll go to bed soon. Mrs Blake is going to pay me threepence an hour to weed the garden! Shall we go and see *Captain Hornblower* next week? Gregory Peck's in it!

Matey   Good idea.

Paul   I wonder which books they've used for it.

Matey   Are you hungry?

Paul   Yes, sir! Do you think it's a good night for a midnight feast?

Matey   An excellent night.

Paul   Let me tell you a secret, Matey! I'm going to declare war on Mr Edwards!

Matey   Really?

Paul   I'm going to have to stand up for myself. More than I have done. There won't be anything left of me if I don't. They're all wearing me down. He's trying to crack my shell. He does it on purpose. I can't stand it much longer. I'll either beat him or I'll run away and never be seen again. I hate him so much, Matey.

Matey   Be patient.

Paul   What's going to happen to Mrs Blake when I go away to school?

Matey   Don't you worry. She's as tough as old boots.

Paul   Sometimes she likes me, sometimes she doesn't. I never know what she's going to be like. She gets angry if I refer to her as my grandmother. I've never ever called her Granny! Is she mad?

Matey   No more than the rest of us.

Paul   She's very odd. Will I be like that one day?

Matey   If you're lucky. Now, my spies tell me that there are some chocolate biscuits not far away!

Paul   I've given up chocolate for Lent. What a fool! I could eat a whole packet of chocolate biscuits right now!

Matey   I don't think chocolate biscuits count, do they?

Paul   I know this is mad, but I've got this fear, that if I break my promise and eat chocolate, it will somehow affect my parents. I mean . . . their resurrection.

Matey   Paul, it would give your parents, both of whom I loved dearly, the greatest pleasure to know that you were eating chocolate biscuits tonight. You eat half the packet, and I'll eat the other half. I think that makes a lot of sense.

Paul   Matey, their bodies must have been smashed to pieces.

The shattering sound of an air crash. **Paul** *screaming.*

Blackout.

Part Two

Harry Mortimer playing Haydn's Trumpet Concerto second movement.

Mr Edwards *is painting in the garden. It is a beautiful day.* **Paul** *watches him quietly.*

Mr Edwards Why don't you do something useful?

Paul I am, sir.

Mr Edwards Why don't you weed the garden?

Paul I did, sir. All morning.

Mr Edwards Where's Mr Maitland?

Paul In 2A, sir. Painting the blackboard. Do you mind me watching you, sir?

Mr Edwards Not if you're quiet.

Paul I am quiet, sir. I only talk if you ask me something.

Mr Edwards Have you seen my dear wife?

Paul She went for a walk . . . after we had finished the dishes, sir.

Mr Edwards Where?

Paul The Bluebell Woods, sir.

Mr Edwards Good.

Paul Yes . . . would you like a sweet, sir?

Mr Edwards No thank you.

Paul They're extra strong mints, sir. You said you liked extra strong mints.

Mr Edwards When?

Paul   In Scripture. Last term. We were doing the marriage feast at Cana. Jesus had just turned the water into wine, sir, and you said you liked extra strong mints after a meal. Mallet said that if he'd been at the marriage feast, and he'd been offered an extra strong mint, he'd have asked Jesus to turn it into fudge! You threw chalk at him and actually hit him, sir! We all believed in miracles after that!

Mr Edwards   Are you trying to stop me painting, Blake?

Paul   No, sir! I was offering you a sweet, sir. It's a jolly good painting, sir. Which tree is it?

Mr Edwards   The silver birch.

Paul   It's a weeping silver birch. It's a very sad tree!

Mr Edwards   Shut up, Blake.

Paul   Yes, sir.

Mr Edwards   Blake?

Paul   Yes, sir.

Mr Edwards   Would you do me a kindness?

Paul   Yes, sir.

Mr Edwards   Would you fill that up with fresh water for me?

Paul   Yes, sir . . . hot or cold, sir?

Mr Edwards   Cold.

Paul   Yes, sir. How full, sir?

Mr Edwards   Nearly up to the top.

Paul   Yes, sir . . . are you sure you wouldn't like a sweet, sir?

Mr Edwards   No thank you, Blake!

Paul   OK!

Paul *leaves.* **Mrs Edwards** *arrives, trailing ivy from the woods.*

Mrs Edwards   I thought a little ivy would brighten the place up.

Mr Edwards   How considerate of you.

Mrs Edwards   This is one of those days when it's actually good to be alive!

Mr Edwards   I'm sorry, my love.

Mrs Edwards   Bernard! I've got to talk to you. Now put down your brush! You failed to strip your bed this morning! You know how important it is to air your sheets properly. I've explained this to you time and time again. It's a nasty, unhealthy habit! The boys get into serious trouble from me and matron if they fail to strip their beds before breakfast. You know that perfectly well!

Mr Edwards   I'm very sorry, my dear.

Mrs Edwards   And you left your wet towel lying on the bathroom floor. What on earth has come over you? I thought I had you properly trained. The older you get, the more slovenly you become!

Mr Edwards   May I get on with my painting?

Mrs Edwards   Your beastly painting! You paint that miserable tree every year. You know I always use your paintings to light the boiler. It's a thorough waste of time and money! Those wretched boys are having a bad influence on you. Only the stupidest boys take art lessons. I really find it humiliating to see you sitting there, looking so ridiculous. In fact it is presumptuous! If you had any talent at all, that might go some way towards compensating for my embarrassment. But you haven't! You know you haven't! I've told you you haven't! Why do you persist year after year in this idle, effeminate pursuit?

Paul *comes back with the fresh paint water.*

Paul   There you are, sir.

Mrs Edwards   Don't burst into other people's conversations. You rude boy! Go away! *Go away!*

Paul *leaves.*

Mrs Edwards You must do something about that boy!
I've told you a thousand times! It's your responsibility.

Mr Edwards *sips the paint water patiently.*

Mrs Edwards The discipline in the school is slipping
atrociously! It starts at the top.

Mr Edwards Shouldn't you be thinking about preparing
tea, my pet?

Mrs Edwards I am thinking about it. I know my duties.
Now pack up your things, go upstairs and tidy your bedroom!

Mr Edwards I'll do it later.

Mrs Edwards Please do it now . . . if you love me!

Mr Edwards Very well.

Mrs Edwards *goes off to the kitchen.* **Mr Edwards** *gathers up his
things and sets off towards the house.*

End of second movement of Haydn's Trumpet Concerto.

Paul *and* **Matey** *are playing pontoon in 2A.*

Paul Twist. Twist again. Bust!

Matey *takes the stake money and deals again.*

Paul *(looking at his first card)* Threepence!

He puts down his stake money.

Matey *(looking at his card)* Double!

Paul Good!

Paul *puts down another threepence in stake money.* **Matey** *deals out
another card to* **Paul** *and himself.* **Paul** *looks at his card.*

Paul Buy for sixpence!

He puts the money down.

Matey I thought that we agreed that threepence was the
highest stake.

Paul You've doubled. I can buy for sixpence in this round.

Matey *deals* **Paul** *another card face down.* **Paul** *looks at it.*

Paul   Buy for another six!

He puts another sixpence onto the pile of stake money.

Matey   I thought you were broke.

Paul   There's money in weeds.

Matey   What are you doing?

Paul   Wait a bit.

Paul *counts up the total number of points he is holding in his four cards.*

Paul   Buy for another six! Please . . . *please* . . .

Matey *deals out another card face down.* **Paul** *picks it up.*

Paul   YESSSSSSSS! Five-card trick! I've won! I'm rich!
I'M RICH!!!

Matey   Let me see.

Paul   Twenty-one exactly!

Matey   You mangy litle creep!

Paul   A five carder! That's five times the stake money!
That's ten shillings you owe me. TEN SHILLINGS!

Matey   Now hold on!

Matey *turns over his cards.*

I might get a five carder.

He turns over another card.

That's ten . . .

He turns over a fourth card.

That's seventeen . . .

Paul   You can't do this to me, Matey!

Matey *turns over a fifth card.*

Paul   BUST! You're bust, Matey!

Matey   Damn!

Paul Ten shillings!

Matey That's a whole hour's work.

Paul Do you get ten bob an hour for mending desks?

Matey Yes.

Paul That's not fair.

Matey *gives* **Paul** *ten shillings*.

Matey There you are. Always pay your debts.

Paul Gosh! Thank you, sir!

Matey Right! Now, I think you should let me get on with my work.

Paul It's almost staff tea time.

Matey Good grief.

Paul I'll tell you what, Matey. We'll go and see *The Sign of Pagan* AND I'll pay!

Matey There's no need for that.

Paul Please, Matey. I'd like to. Let's go tomorrow!

Matey We'll see.

Paul *Please*, Matey! The trailer was terrific! Even you said so. There's a tremendous amount of fighting in it. Let's go tomorrow. I promise I'll pay. You can have an ice cream as well. *Please*, Matey! We can get there in time for the newsreel.

Matey I'll talk to your grandmother. Now push off!

Paul OK . . . I'm pushing off!

Matey Well push off, then!

Paul *I am pushing off*! Please, Matey . . .

Matey I'm going for tea, damn it.

Paul Shall we play cricket after staff tea, Matey? I'll bowl to you. You can bat first. It's a smashing evening for nets, sir.

Matey Right! I'll see you at the nets at a quarter to five. *Now push off*!!!

Paul   Thank you, sir!

Paul *pushes off*.

Matey   Damn it! Damn it!

He leaves for staff tea.

Isobel Baillie singing 'My Heart Ever Faithful'.

Paul *is drinking a mug of tea on his own.*

Paul   In term time, tea is put out on the trolly in Little
School. That's in the summer term. We have supper in the
dining-hall later on. We can spend more time out of doors
after lessons that way. Matey has to have tea in the staff room,
even though he's on his own. Mrs Edwards puts mine out on
the trolley, even in the holidays. I've been playing through
the school records a lot. Isobel Baillie is good. Mr Stroud, the
music teacher, says we've got to sing 'My Heart Ever
Faithful' like she does. Roberts does quite a good imitation,
but his voice is starting to break. Mrs Edwards never puts
enough sugar in the tea. She says she does, but we're always
complaining. I'm going to get stumps and pads from the
pavillion. I know where all the keys are kept.

He leaves.

Mr Edwards *is visiting* **Mrs Blake** *on school matters.*

Mrs Blake   Why have you put Sanky into 3B? He's far too
clever. His father won't be amused.

Mr Edwards   He only got 37% in the maths exam. His
form master's report suggests that some remedial work is
necessary.

Mrs Blake   Sanky read to the other boys in the dormitory
for most of last term. He read *Treasure Island* most beautifully.
Beautifully! I won't hear of it. He must be in 3A! He must!

Mr Edwards   Then someone will have to move down to
3B. There's only room for nineteen desks in 3A, Mrs Blake.

Mrs Blake   Parker! He doesn't wash properly. He's lazy.

Mr Edwards   Parker . . . Parker . . . quite good at Latin . . . poor French . . . average mathematics . . . poor spelling . . .

Mrs Blake   3B!

Mr Edwards   Very well.

Mrs Blake   I think I am satisfied with the other class lists you have prepared, Mr Edwards.

Mr Edwards   I'm going to speak my mind, Mrs Blake. It is now two years since you asked me, as senior master, to assume your late son's position as headmaster.

Mrs Blake   Two years . . .

Mr Edwards   I feel . . . my wife feels . . . I mean . . . I feel you must permit me to have a greater say in the running of the school. I am deeply concerned about the way things are going here. I must be able to make decisions without having to keep coming to you to have them ratified. I cannot carry on like this. It's bad for the school, it's bad for the morale of the staff. In the remaining years that I have before my retirement, I do wish to take control. I mean . . . in an appropriate manner.

Mrs Blake   So you're accusing me of interfering?

Mr Edwards   We know you have the interests of the school at heart.

Mrs Blake   You fool!

Mr Edwards   I hope you don't mind me . . .

Mrs Blake   I've kept it going all these years with my money! You know that! Disgraceful man! Shocking! You'd cram all the classes full of boys if you could. I know the games you and your dear wife are up to.

Mr Edwards   What games?

Mrs Blake   I know about the books you order for yourself out of school money. I know about the private accounts you have both been using for your own purposes. In a moment of crisis, I placed you above your station. My husband would have had a fit if he had known that you would one day become headmaster! A fit! However, I think this is the right moment to tell you that I am advertising for a new headmaster. A younger man. To take over after the summer term.

Mr Edwards   This is outrageous!

Mrs Blake   I have already contacted Gabbitas and Thring!

Mr Edwards   My God!

Mrs Blake   I shall interview candidates myself during next term. I want you and your wife to retire. I shall pay you in full up to your sixty-fifth birthday, so you will have a steady income until then. I shall pay your wife a lump sum in the autumn, when the fees come in. You won't lose a penny by this arrangement.

Mr Edwards   I won't let you do this!

Mrs Blake   Don't raise your arm at me!

Mr Edwards   We won't be cast out like this! After all we've done! You stupid, treacherous woman!

Mrs Blake   That's enough!

Mr Edwards   You don't know what you're doing! There would be no need for me to retire, even at sixty-five. I'm perfectly fit.

Mrs Blake   I don't wish to discuss this matter any further with you now.

Mr Edwards   It's you who should move out! *You*! You refuse to listen to sensible advice. You should have sent the boy away two years ago.

Mrs Blake   We're not discussing him, Edwards.

Mr Edwards   I said so then, didn't I? Didn't I?

Mrs Blake   How you'd love to get us both out of the way! How you'd love to rule the roost! I'll see there's a proper man in charge before I'm gone. You've never fooled me for one instant. You've held the fort for two years. For that I'm grateful. I intend to see that you are correctly rewarded. You'll end your career at the top, and it was me that put you there. Be grateful, Edwards!

Mr Edwards   You can't get rid of me that easily.

Mrs Blake   Don't make a total fool of yourself.

Mr Edwards   The staff are entirely behind me.

Mrs Blake   Ha!

Mr Edwards   My wife will be furious!

Mrs Blake   Yes!

Mr Edwards   I'm not finished yet.

Mrs Blake   In the last few minutes you have called me stupid . . . treacherous! You have behaved in the most threatening manner. I don't think we have a lot left to say to one another. I'll keep my word. You'll get your money. From now on, I insist that we conclude our business together in a correct fashion. You will have no complaints.

Mr Edwards   My God! We'll see!

Mr Edwards *storms out.*

Paul *and* **Matey** *have finished their nets. They are sitting in the evening sun with their cricket things.*

Matey   Let's hope that we have one of those beautiful summers with good, firm wickets . . . when the ball comes swiftly onto the bat.

Paul   Do you think Walton should be wicket keeper? I mean instead of Butcher? I think he should. He stands up to the wicket more than Butcher, even when Stanley's bowling! Stanley's going to be really fast this year. I think he's terrific, don't you?

Matey   He's a good bowler.

Paul   We should beat Brocklehurst. We should thrash them. And Prior's Court. They were useless last year.

Matey That's entirely the wrong attitude. Never underestimate the opposition. Prior's Court had a fine looking Second XI. They'll be good this season. You'll have your work cut out. And, young Paul, you're getting some very bad habits!

Paul What am I doing?

Matey You try that leg glance off your pads too often.

Paul *picks up his bat and plays the stroke.*

Matey That's the one. You've got an excellent eye. I'm not trying to put you off playing good strokes. But if you keep playing that one to straight balls, you're going to get out LBW far too often.

Paul I like that shot.

Matey There's no need to play it when a conventional defensive stroke would be a far safer bet. When your eye is in and you're chasing runs against good bowling . . . that's the time to use it.

Paul *plays a backward then a forward defensive stroke.*

Matey That's more like it. Why take unnecessary risks? Play the straight balls carefully. It's as simple as that.

Paul It's really warm.

Matey You haven't told anyone what I told you the other night.

Paul Of course not. I promised.

Matey You haven't told Mrs Blake?

Paul No.

Matey Good boy.

Paul Sir . . .

Matey What?

Paul Sir . . . you know Mr Edwards talks to the boys when they leave . . . you know . . . the leavers' talk . . . well . . . what does he say?

Matey   How should I know?

Paul   You do know. I'm sure you do.

Matey   He gives them all an old boys' tie.

Paul   There's more to it than that, sir.

Matey   He shakes hands and wishes them good luck at their public schools . . . and tells them not to let the side down.

Paul   Why won't anyone tell me? I know it's about the facts of life. I feel stupid not knowing about things. Nobody tells you anything at this school.

Matey   I doubt very much whether Edwards is an authority on the facts of life, dear boy. When I was a boy, we learnt such things in the dormitory at nights.

Paul   Did you? Did you really, Matey?

Matey   Well . . . I mean . . . not exactly . . . some things . . .

Paul   I have learnt some things. Some quite dirty things. But I still don't understand. I can't make sense of it all. I don't like growing up. I've been perfectly happy the way I am. I don't want to grow up. I think hair on your body is ugly. Trevis used to be quite nice, but he's become hairy . . . you know . . . round his thing . . . I don't like him any more. I don't want to change. Why do things keep happening to you that spoil everything?

Matey   Oh God! Let's talk about cricket.

Paul   I don't want to talk about cricket.

Matey   Growing up isn't as bad as all that. There are compensations.

Paul   Well what the hell are they? What are they, sir?

Matey   Wait and see. Be patient!

Paul   I've got a secret.

Matey   Oh?

Paul   Do you promise not to tell anybody?

Matey All right.

Paul Do you promise?

Matey I promise.

Paul I started getting hairy.

Matey Oh?

Paul I shaved myself clean with Daddy's razor.

Matey *wants to laugh.*

Paul I don't think that's in the least funny.

Matey I'm sorry, Paul. You're the most dear boy and I love you very much.

Matey *starts to laugh.*

Paul It isn't funny!

Matey It is quite funny!

Paul *picks up his cricket bat and starts to play strokes with it.*

Paul It isn't! It isn't! *It isn't!*

Matey No. It isn't really.

Matey *can't control himself and starts to laugh again.*

Paul Matey!

Matey I'm sorry. Come and sit down. Come on!

Paul I know it's silly, but it isn't funny!

Matey The secret is . . . there's nothing to be frightened of.

Paul That's not a secret.

Matey I just don't want to talk about it, so just forget it.

Paul How can I?

Matey It's not for me to talk about such things. The housemaster at your public school will tell you what you want to know when the time is right.

Paul How do you know?

Matey   They always do. You're too young. We really shouldn't be talking about such things.

Paul   We aren't talking about anything.

Matey   I can't do it, Paul. Please understand. I don't know how to start. Now please stop it. It's such a beautiful evening. Don't spoil it. There's a good boy.

Paul   Everything's mad.

Matey   Yes.

Paul   Have you got any prisoner-of-war books?

Matey   No.

Paul   I mean . . . the sort of books that aren't in the school library.

Matey   No.

Paul   You could find the right sort of books for me to read, Matey.

Matey   Mrs Blake would have a fit.

Paul   I wouldn't show her.

Matey   Would you gather up the balls? And take the stumps over to the pavillion?

Paul   Are you going?

Matey   It's getting a bit chilly. I think I'll take a quick bath before supper.

He gets ready to go.

Paul   What are you doing tonight?

Matey   That's my business.

Paul   Are you going out?

Matey   There are ten balls, Blake. There's the bag.

Matey *leaves.*

Paul *gathers all the cricket gear and sets off towards the pavillion.*

The opening of the second movement of Beethoven's Fourth Piano Concerto, played by Schnabel.

Mr *and* **Mrs Edwards** *together*.

Mrs Edwards   I told you years ago you should have had a contract.

Mr Edwards   None of the staff have contracts. You don't have a contract.

Mrs Edwards   I can see you're ready to give in. Typical! Weak! We should take legal advice tomorrow.

Mr Edwards   My dear, I have spent the last half hour on the phone.

Mrs Edwards   Well?

Mr Edwards   We mustn't do anything rash. Stay calm. Time is still on our side.

Mrs Edwards   Time? We have nowhere to go. No house. Nothing.

Mr Edwards   We've received nothing in writing. No dates. No terms of settlement.

Mrs Edwards   Her mind doesn't work like that. Get the doctor in. Have her certified insane. She's not capable of making decisions.

Mr Edwards   She owns everything.

Mrs Edwards   She owns nothing! She's merely a trustee for the boy.

Mr Edwards   Consider for a moment what we might get if we go along with her intentions. I'll be retired on full pay for another two years. I'll be getting various annuities and a pension. You will be getting an undisclosed sum. If we really put the pressure on, I think we'll persuade her to buy us a house somewhere. Suddenly, after forty years of Gorse Park, no more class lists, fortnightly orders, reports, parents meetings, Sports Days, no more homesickness, bed wetting, dormitories in quarantine! For you, no more laundry, cooking for the ungrateful staff, no more midnight watches on the store cupboard to see who's pinching the rations! I'm beginning to like the idea! We can travel. You can go to Scotland. I can go to France. Haven't we done quite well?

Mrs Edwards   Kill the bitch!

Mr Edwards   What?

Mrs Edwards   Murder!

Mr Edwards   What?

Mrs Edwards   What a wonderful chance! Wouldn't it give you pleasure to watch her die? After all these years of abuse. Oh . . . she thinks herself mighty important! There are some debts that must be paid. I have been so polite, so cunning. I have humiliated myself to her so often. She calls me Frances as though I was a friend. I know she despises me. I heard her once say how well we'd done, considering we were just ordinary people!

Mr Edwards   What are you saying? My dear, you need a rest.

Mrs Edwards   Help me do it!

Mr Edwards   We wouldn't gain anything. We'd lose out on a lot of money. We should do everything in our power to keep her alive until the end of the summer term! After that, she can drop dead whenever she likes. Where are you going?

Mrs Edwards   Mrs Blake wants her beef tea.

Mr Edwards   I don't think she really wants it tonight.

Mrs Edwards   Of course she does.

Mr Edwards   You've worked so hard today. Let me make it. Please sit down!

Mrs Edwards   Don't fuss, Bernard. I know my duty.

Mr Edwards   I really do think we should talk further about this.

Mrs Edwards   Get out of my way!

Mr Edwards   I'll come and help you, my dear.

They leave for the kitchen.

The Gypsy Rondo from Haydn's Piano Trio Op. 73 No. 2 played by Cortot, Thibaud and Casals.

Paul *and* **Mrs Blake** *are concluding a hand of 'Honeymoon Bridge'. The dummy hands are held by special wooden blocks, so that you cannot see your opponent's dummy hand.*

Paul   I think I'll try this way round.

Mrs Blake   Hmmmmm . . .

Paul *plays another trick and wins with a finesse.*

Paul   Good-oh!

Mrs Blake   Oh foolish boy!

Paul *plays another trick and then another, to complete the hand.*

Paul   Bid three no trumps. Made four!

Paul *adds up the score.*

That's rubber to me . . . by 720 points!

Mrs Blake   That's sevenpence I owe you.

She searches in her purse.

There you are!

Paul   Thank you, Mrs Blake.

Mrs Blake   You're improving.

Paul   Why did you call me 'oh foolish boy'?

Mrs Blake   There was no need to finesse my queen of diamonds. It would have fallen prey to your king anyway. You must count your cards.

Paul   I thought there were two diamonds still out.

Mrs Blake   I discarded a diamond when you were playing out the spades.

Paul Oh!

Mrs Blake Never mind. You played the rest of the rubber very well. There's another sixpence.

Paul Thank you very much.

Mrs Blake Dear boy!

Paul Have you had enough?

Mrs Blake Quite enough!

Paul I've prepared the Dickens questions.

Paul *gets out a sheet of paper.*

Mrs Blake Splendid! I'll give you a penny for every one I get wrong!

Paul First lines. I want you to tell me the name of the book.

Mrs Blake Good.

Paul 'Although I am an old man, night is generally my time for walking.'

Mrs Blake Ahhh! Now that is *The Old Curiosity Shop*.

Paul Right. 'There once lived, in a sequestered part of the county of Devonshire, one . . . ' Who lived in a sequestered part of the county of Devonshire? And which book?

Mrs Blake Hmmmmmm! The book is *Nicholas Nickleby*. And the man is . . . now it's Mr something Nickleby . . . Godfrey! Godfrey Nickleby!

Paul Very good, Mrs Blake!

Mrs Blake Dickens has the most wonderful way of leading you into a story. Did you notice that in *The Old Curiosity Shop* you are not quite sure at first who is telling the story?

Paul I only read the first bit.

Mrs Blake As soon as Easter is over, you shall read it to me. We'll read it to each other!

Paul Good.

Mrs Blake It's very sad. *Very* sad! Your grandfather gave me that set of Dickens when we got married. He was a very shrewd man! We went to Brighton for our honeymoon. We read *The Pickwick Papers* together. He was very clever with all the voices. He was a very clever actor. We used to put on all sorts of plays. The boys loved him. *Loved* him! He was an absolute *panic*!

Paul Who bought the school? Where did you used to live?

Mrs Blake My husband came from Somerset. He taught at the local church school. His father was a farmer. I had money from my side of the family. I bought Gorse Park and we started our own school. We wanted the boys to be part of the family. We thought forty boys was quite enough. Your father was born here.

Paul I wasn't, was I . . .

Mrs Blake Your mother went into hospital. That night there was an air raid and they bombed Reading. Your mother always said you came into the world with a bang!

Paul Did she?

Mrs Blake Do you want to become headmaster here, one day?

Paul I don't know.

Mrs Blake I mean long after I've been gathered in. When you're a man.

Paul I can't think that far ahead. I've got to go away to boarding school, worse luck.

Mrs Blake Yes.

Paul I'd like to own it, when the time comes. But that doesn't have to mean that I'm headmaster, does it?

Mrs Blake No.

Paul I can decide later, can't I?

Mrs Blake I know I haven't always treated you fairly . . .
no . . . don't interrupt! But with the time I've got left, I want to
see that you get what is rightfully yours.

Paul Mr Maitland is getting quite old. He's always been
very kind to me. When I go away, can he stay on here as long
as he likes? He hasn't got any other home to go to.

Mrs Blake I'll tell you a secret. He's over seventy!

Paul Golly!

Mrs Blake There will always be a job for him here. If he
wants to stop taking classes, I'll put him in charge of the
library. What do you think of that?

Paul You'll have to ask him first.

Mrs Blake True.

Paul But he'll be able to stay?

Mrs Blake As long as he wishes.

Paul Thank you.

Mrs Blake Now! I'm ready for bed!

Paul Wait a moment. 'Thirty years ago, Marseilles lay
burning in the sun, one day.'

Mrs Blake *Little Dorrit.* Now be an angel and tell that
dreadful Mrs Edwards that I don't want any beef tea tonight.

Paul Right oh!

She goes off to bed.

Paul *leaves for the kitchen.*

Paul (*off*) Good night!

Mrs Blake (*off*) Don't be late!

Paul (*off*) I won't!

Mrs Edwards *is tottering through the school with a cup of beef tea.*
Mr Edwards *is close behind her.*

Mr Edwards She's bound to have gone to bed by now.

Mrs Edwards   Stop fussing!

Mr Edwards   Let me take it up.

Mrs Edwards   There's nothing in it!

Mr Edwards   I don't trust you!

Paul *meets them.*

Mrs Edwards   You should be in bed!

Paul   Mrs Blake says she doesn't want any Bovril tonight.

Mrs Edwards   Rubbish!

Paul   She doesn't!

Mr Edwards   I told you so.

Mrs Edwards (*to her husband*)   Would you like this?

Mr Edwards   No.

Mrs Edwards (*to* **Paul**)   You've been looking rather pale lately, Paul. Why not take this up to bed with you?

Paul   I hate the stuff.

Matey *returns from the local pub.*

Matey   Is this the party?

Mr Edwards   Good evening, Maitland.

Matey (*quoting Kipling*)
This is the hour of pride and power
Talon and tush and claw
Oh hear the call!
Good hunting all
That keep the Jungle Law!

Mrs Edwards   You've been drinking! I can smell it from here!

Matey
Look thy den is hid and deep
Lest a wrong by thee forgot,
Draw thy killer to the spot.

Mr Edwards   My dear, I think you better take that back. (*The drink.*)

Mrs Edwards (*to* **Matey**)   Take this. It'll do you good.

Matey
Wood and water, wind and tree
Wisdom, strength and courtesy
Jungle-favour go with thee!

Matey *takes the cup of beef tea.*

Mrs Edwards   The cheese is locked away.

Matey   Howl, dogs! A *wolf* has died tonight!

Mr Edwards   Mr Maitland!

Matey   Sir?

Mr Edwards   Go to bed!

Matey *leaves, there's a crash.*

Paul   I'll see if he's all right.

Mrs Edwards   Stay there! Beastly child!

Matey *comes back with a broken cup and saucer.*

Matey   Sorry about that!

Mrs Edwards   Clumsy idiot!

Paul   Are you OK?

Matey   Perfectly. Good night!

He leaves.

Mrs Edwards (*to* **Paul**)   *Go to bed*!!

Paul *leaves.*

Mrs Edwards   Damn!

Mr Edwards   You need a good, long sleep.

Mrs Edwards   Humm!

They leave.

*Sir Edward Elgar conducting the slumber scene from The Wand of
Youth Suite No. 1.*

It is Easter morning. **Mrs Blake** *is sitting, almost asleep, in the
garden on another beautiful day. She has picked a basketful of daffodils.*
Paul, *wearing his Sunday best clothes, is sitting nearby, reading a
book.*

Matey *comes from the house with a tray of sherry glasses and two
decanters of sherry. He too has his Sunday best clothes on.*

Paul   Matey's here.

Mrs Blake   Thank God!

Matey   The head will be coming shortly.

Mrs Blake   Do serve the sherry. I'm absolutely gasping.

Matey   Sweet or dry, Mrs Blake?

Mrs Blake   Sweet, please.

Matey *pours her a large glassful.*

Mrs Blake   My dear! How wonderful! Now do help
yourself, Matey.

Paul   Can I have some, Mrs Blake?

Mrs Blake   *May I*!

Paul   *May* I have some, please?

Mrs Blake   You hate sherry.

Paul   I don't. It is Easter day. Please?

Mrs Blake   Do you think we should, Mr Maitland?

Matey   I did bring him a glass, Mrs Blake.

Mrs Blake   My dear! Which would you like? Which would
he like, Matey?

Matey   I think he'd better start with the sweet.

Mrs Blake   So do I.

Matey *pours* **Paul** *a glass and gives it to him.*

Paul   Thanks, Matey.

Paul *sips it and chokes slightly.*

Mrs Blake Silly boy!

Paul It went up my nose.

Matey Well . . . I'd like to wish you all a very happy Easter!

Mrs Blake Happy Easter!

Paul Happy Easter!

They drink.

Mrs Blake Do sit down, Matey. Wasn't the vicar dreadful! So gloomy! He will mumble!

Paul Mrs Blake, if you were a prisoner of war, how would you escape?

Mrs Blake I would never allow myself to be captured! Those beastly Germans! What on earth are you reading?

Paul *The Naked Island.*

Mrs Blake Most unsuitable!

Paul It's good.

Mrs Blake It sounds disgusting! Do put it away. At once!

Paul Where are Daddy's stamp albums?

Mrs Blake Not now . . .

Paul They are safe, aren't they?

Mrs Blake Perfectly.

Paul Can I see them?

Mrs Blake They're locked away.

Paul May I see them after lunch?

Mrs Blake You're not in the least interested in stamps any more! You sold most of your collection to Pettigrew two terms ago.

Paul   I wanted to buy lights for the puppet theatre. I've got to get money somehow. I didn't want to sell them. Mr Edwards took the first day covers that Daddy sent me.

Mrs Blake   Rubbish!

Paul   He did! He gave me half a crown for the lot. I could have got ten bob from Pettigrew. Mr Edwards swindled me! That's why I left the Stamp Club. I was really angry with myself. The first day covers were the best part of my collection. Once they were gone, there didn't seem much point in keeping the rest. I would like to see Daddy's stamps. Just to see them.

Mrs Blake   And how are the desks? Have you been round every classroom?

Matey   I've just got 3B to do.

Paul   3B! You must be careful when you get to Sleigh-Jones's desk. Sleigh-Jones made the best marble slide in the school last term, and he asked me to take care of it in the holidays. There's a hole where the inkwell goes, and you put a marble in there, and it travels for forty-seven seconds around the inside of the desk before it drops out of a hole in the bottom! It's brilliant! Please don't move his desk around too much, Matey.

Mr *and* **Mrs Edwards** *arrive.*

Mrs Blake   My dears! Do come and join us! Matey! Mrs Edwards loves her sherry as dry as possible. Isn't it heavenly?

Mrs Edwards   I see you've wiped out the last of the daffodils.

Mrs Blake   Do give her a *large* glassful.

Mr Edwards   Sweet for me, Maitland.

Matey *serves out the drinks.*

Paul   Could I try some of the dry now, please?

Mrs Blake   You haven't drunk it all already? You wicked boy!

Mr Edwards   Have you been drinking?

Mrs Blake   I gave him permission.

Mr Edwards   I see.

Mrs Edwards   You're far too young to drink. Matron would have a fit!

Paul   Yes, she would! I'd like to see what the dry tastes like.

Mr Edwards   You've had quite enough.

Paul   I only want a small amount.

Mrs Blake   Give him a drop, Matey. Only a drop!

Mrs Edwards   He won't eat his lunch.

Paul   I will.

Matey *gives* **Paul** *a small amount of the dry sherry.*

Mrs Blake   Now then, no more squabbling! Be happy everyone!

Paul   I'm exquisitely happy.

Mrs Blake   Good! How's the lunch going, Frances?

Mrs Edwards   Everything is in hand.

Paul   I'd rather have mine on a plate!

Mrs Blake   Shut up! My dear Bernard, do tell us how your painting is coming along.

Mr Edwards   It would be easier if people would leave me alone.

Mrs Blake   Absolutely. He's so very talented. I can see painting becoming the chief delight of his old age.

Paul   Next to Mrs Edwards.

Mrs Blake   Be quiet!

Mr Edwards   The roll for next term comes to 104 boys!

Mrs Blake   Oh?

Mrs Edwards   Well done!

Mr Edwards   I didn't want to have to turn down twins, and there are three more boys in the family. It's a great pity we cannot create a new classroom. The demand is there. Our other facilities could cope with 120 boys without unnecessary strain. We wouldn't even have to engage extra staff. The greatly increased income would be useful for building a science room in the conservatory.

Mrs Blake   I don't think we want to talk shop on this occasion. Besides, there isn't room for another classroom.

Mr Edwards   Surely Mr Maitland's room will become available at the end of the summer term?

Paul   It won't!

Mrs Blake   There is no question of Mr Maitland leaving us at the end of the summer. I will not allow this conversation to proceed.

Mrs Edwards   I'm sure it is not your intention to strangle the future.

Mrs Blake   This is a social occasion. The lilac really has been heavenly this year. And I adore the perennial poppies. Aren't they delightful?

Paul   You aren't leaving us, are you, Matey?

Matey   Not as far as I know.

Paul   Good!

Mrs Blake   Paul! Be an angel and go to the woods!

Paul   Do I have to?

Mrs Blake   Pick a bunch of wild flowers, and some bluebells, and some good foliage. Don't bring any more poison ivy! Mrs Edwards very kindly brought quite enough of that in the other day! Now off you go!

Paul *leaves for the woods.*

Mrs Blake   And don't get your best clothes dirty!

Mr Edwards   Decisions have to be made, Mrs Blake.

Mrs Blake I'm surprised at you, Edwards! In front of the boy! And you really owe poor Matey some sort of explanation.

Matey I quite understand. There's no need.

Mrs Edwards I speak for my husband!

Mr Edwards My dear . . .

Mrs Edwards We're not going to be pushed out at the end of the summer! You're a foolish, stupid old woman!

Mrs Blake That's enough!

Mrs Edwards You're certifiably insane!

Mrs Blake *Rot*.

Matey You've said enough, Mrs Edwards.

Mrs Edwards Keep out of my way!

Matey Headmaster! Please do something!

Mrs Blake Thank you, Mr Maitland. I can take care of this.

Mr Edwards My dear, I believe the lunch needs attending to.

Mrs Edwards Let it burn!

Mrs Blake I have stood quite enough of this. I am acting with the full support of the trustees of the estate. Let me make it clear, once and for all! Mr and Mrs Edwards! You *will* be leaving, under the generous terms that I have discussed with Mr Edwards. And I strongly urge you both to behave with dignity in this matter. A settlement worth many thousands of pounds will be made in your favour, most of which will come from my resources, not the school's. I therefore make the entirely reasonable request that you both behave politely, especially in front of staff and pupils. Your affairs here will be settled with generosity and honour! Mr Maitland, would you be so kind as to help Mrs Edwards carry in the food for lunch?

Matey Certainly, Mrs Blake.

Mrs Edwards (*to* **Matey**)   Stay away from me!

Matey   Very well. I'll wait in the dining-room and you can carry it in.

Matey *and* **Mrs Edwards** *leave for the house.*

Mrs Blake   My dear Edwards, please sit down.

Mrs Blake *fills up his sherry glass.*

Mrs Blake   It was never my intention to humiliate you. I'm acting firmly in the interests of everyone, including yourselves. Have you thought further about where you might live?

Mr Edwards   I have always wanted a house near the sea. Perhaps on the south coast, looking across towards France.

Mrs Blake   Then you shall have it! Will you, and Mrs Edwards, spend a week away, at my expense, and find what you are looking for? I shall also be pleased to provide the first £500 towards the cost of the house, in addition to the settlement that I have already outlined.

Mr Edwards   That is most generous. I shall take Frances away for a week.

Mrs Blake   Good. Daylight at last! There are two things that I shall request of you in return.

Mr Edwards   Oh?

Mrs Blake   No more rows. Dignity!

Mr Edwards   What else?

Mrs Blake   Please return the stamps . . . I mean specifically the first day covers that you bought, quite properly, from my grandson at the Stamp Club.

Mr Edwards   Very well.

Mrs Blake   Thank you, Bernard. Drink up. Lunch time, I think. (*She picks up her basket of flowers.*) Poor daffodils! May I take your arm?

Mrs Blake *takes* **Mr Edwards**' *arm and they set off for the house together.*

The Nocturne from A Midsummer Night's Dream *with Dennis Brain's horn; Philharmonia Orchestra conducted by Paul Kletzki.*

Matey'*s room late that night.*

Paul *knocks on the door.*

Matey   Come in.

Paul *enters in his dressing-gown and slippers. He is carrying two stamp albums.*

Paul   I'm sorry to call on you so late, sir.

Matey   It's a quarter to ten. You should be asleep.

Paul   Well I'm not.

Matey   What is it?

Paul   I wanted to talk to you. I wanted to show you something.

Matey   Sit down.

Paul   Thank you, sir.

Matey   Get on with it.

Paul   Here are two of my father's stamp albums.

Matey   Oh.

Paul   I wanted to show them to you.

Matey   Thank you.

Paul *gives him one of the albums.*

Paul   Mrs Blake says he specialised. They're all British.

Matey   I remember him collecting some of these. He had the idea that it was worth collecting whole sheets of stamps. It's important to keep these in a dry place.

Paul   I know. Some of the sheets are stuck together. How do you get them apart again?

Matey   Ahh. Penny Blacks . . . quite a few!

Paul   And Penny Reds.

Matey   Have you tried looking them up in Stanley Gibbons?

Paul   I haven't had time yet. I was wondering if you could explain how to measure perforations.

Matey   Quite simple. Hold the stamp up to the gauge and start counting. I think the secret is not to try and do it too fast. Too many boys guess at the answer. Take your time, Paul.

Paul   Here are some of his Commonwealth stamps.

Paul *passes over the other book.*

Matey   Oh yes . . . yes . . .

Paul   I like the Canadian stamps best.

Matey   They're very beautiful. A very beautiful collection, Paul.

Paul   I've decided that I'm going to keep it going. Mrs Blake says she'll give me a new stamp album for my birthday with a surprise in it!

Matey   Good for her!

Paul   There're a lot of countries. Everyone collects British stamps. I'm going to concentrate on the Commonwealth ones.

Matey   Most impressive.

Matey *hands back the albums.*

Thank you.

Paul   Don't tell Mr Edwards I showed you. He's been pestering me for ages. He wants to get his hands on them. He'll swipe some of them for his own collection. I don't know exactly what's here. I wouldn't even know what I'd lost.

Matey   Have you had a go at the Latin papers I gave you?

Paul   I've looked at some of them.

Matey   When are you going to get down to some work?

Paul   Tomorrow, I suppose.

Matey   You don't sound very keen.

Paul   I'm not. I'm sure none of the other boys have to do Latin in the holidays.

Matey   You want to do well, don't you?

Paul   I suppose I do. I don't think I know anything very important. I'm confused by French. I'm quite good at English and Scripture. History's quite good. I wish I could spell better. I like geometry because circles and triangles look so nice. Algebra is like doing secret codes and reminds me of spy stories. Quadratic equations are meaningless. I don't want to go to public school.

Matey   They'll make a man of you.

Paul   It looks as though I'm going to be a man whether I like it or not.

Matey   You'll learn to stick up for yourself.

Paul   How did you feel when you heard they'd dropped the atomic bomb, Matey?

Matey   Good heavens . . .

Paul   Tell me.

Matey   It was like . . . scoring the winning goal in the Cup Final.

Paul   Didn't it frighten you?

Matey   Not at the time. I don't think we understood what had happened.

Paul   It frightens me terribly. Were you a soldier in the First World War?

Matey   You know I was.

Paul   Why don't you tell us about that, instead of doing Latin?

Matey   You wouldn't pass your exams.

Paul   It would be real! Were you ever a prisoner of war?

Matey   No.

Paul   I've read *The Scourge of the Swastika* now. It was fantastic!

Matey   How did you get hold of it?

Paul   From Simpkins' tuck box. He said I could. I don't want to go to school any more, Matey. I want to run away to sea, or be kidnapped! I want to escape but I don't know how.

Matey   Steady down...

Paul   I feel I'm exploding in all directions! I've lots and lots of secret things... secret thoughts. I've hardly told you anything.

Matey   The problem is... there's a limit to the amount I can take on board, dear boy. I'm old. My memory's full of moments... bits of conversations... embarrassments that strike back at you with force after fifty years of silence. There's too much mud in me that's frightened to be disturbed. Just help me to keep the flow of things clear. If I was a young boy, and your friend... as I believe I am... then I would say to you, 'Let's pack our bags tonight and travel to the ends of the earth and back again!'

Paul   Yes!

Matey   But of course I can't say that now. I'm just an old man, Paul.

Paul   I don't care about you being old.

Matey   Do talk to me about something else, or go to bed.

Paul   Oh! I've brought you some of my Easter egg!

Paul *gets some chocolate egg out of his dressing-gown pocket.*

Matey   Thank you.

Paul *breaks a bit and starts to eat it.*

Paul   Aren't you going to try some?

Matey I'll eat it later.

Paul Have some now.

Matey *breaks a bit off his piece of egg and eats it.*

Paul It's not bad, is it . . .

Matey Thank you . . .

Paul I've discovered some more music, Matey!

Matey Oh?

Paul There are only two records left out of the original set.
It's Elgar's violin concerto. Elgar's actually conducting!
There's the slow movement and the end of the last
movement. There used to be six records, Matey. The rest are
lost or bust. The music is very strange, and I don't really
understand it. But I have to keep going back to it. It's really
weird!

Matey And do you know the name of the violinist?

Paul Menuhin.

Matey He was just a little older than you when he made
that recording.

Paul Is he still alive?

Matey Very alive.

Paul And Elgar?

Matey Very dead.

Paul I'm going to search through the record shops and
find the missing records.

Matey If you find any of them buy them, whatever the
price, and I will pay you back. Will you let me do that?

Paul Thank you, sir.

Matey Off you go to bed. And take care of the stamps.

Paul Don't tell Mr Edwards.

Matey No. Off you go.

Paul Thank you, sir.

Paul *leaves.*

Paul *is on his way to bed.*

Paul   In the dormitory, mine's the only bed with a mattress on. I mean in the holidays. On the last morning of term, all the boys carry their mattresses into Ruskin dorm . . . it's above the boiler room. All the other beds in my dorm look like black skeletons at night time! I stubbed my toe on one in the middle of last night. Sometimes I wake up and wonder why it's so quiet. Then in the mornings I lie there in a doze, waiting for Matey to come round with the bell. He makes a terrific noise! He doesn't do it in the holidays, of course. On the last morning of term, we all throw things at him . . . like wet flannels and slippers! It's all terrific fun! There's still two weeks left of the holidays, then the boys' trunks start to turn up, and matron and the domestic staff come back and everything gets cleaned, and the masters turn up. There's a new master next term. There nearly always is.

It's quite embarrassing not being a prefect, even in your last term. Everyone will ask why, and think I've done something wrong. You can't keep explaining that the headmaster is a rotten worm.

At least there's cricket and Music Club and the best ever puppet show. And Matthew Dolan. He's my friend. There's quite a lot to look forward to . . .

The closing bars of the Elgar concerto . . .

Massage

Massage was first performed at the Lyric Studio, Hammersmith, on 6 October 1986, with the following cast:

Rikki, *a massage boy*	Dexter Fletcher
Dodge, *a bicycle builder*	David Allister
Jane, *a journalist*	Pamela Merrick

Directed by Michael Wilcox
Designed by Bernard Culshaw
Lighting by John A. Williams

Part One

*Hammersmith, West London, 1986, Wednesday 27 August, around six
o'clock. The back room of* **Tony Dodge***'s bicycle shop. A workbench
is piled with toys and books belonging to* **Simon***. A skateboard, with
one set of wheels removed, is held upside-down in a vice. The frame of a
new bicycle is held in a jig. Its wheels are missing, but it is otherwise
complete. It has no toe clips. Piles of rubbish and boxes of roughly packed
belongings are scattered around the place.*

*A table has been laid for two. One door leads to the main part of the shop
and the street entrance. Another door leads out of the room into a small
back kitchen. Parts of bicycle frames, old wheels and debris of*
Dodge*'s trade litter the room. There are piles of unopened letters.*

Tony Dodge *enters with his superb, fast-touring bicycle. He is
wearing a cyclist's tracksuit, with cyclist's shorts, shirt and shoes. He
has just dashed to the shops. He picks up his bicycle and hangs it by its
crossbar on a workframe, so that its wheels are well clear of the ground.
He unpacks the small backpack and brings out a bottle of fresh orange
juice and a box of cheap candles. He places two candles in holders on the
table. He fills an empty jug full of the orange juice. He hides his wallet in
its usual hiding-place above one of the workbenches. The shop doorbell
rings.*

Rikki *has walked through the shop to the back room. He comes to the
door of the back room. He is nineteen, from East London, but looks
younger. He has a shoulder bag with his things in it. He has never visited*
Dodge *before.*

Rikki   Mr Dodge?

Dodge   Come in.

Rikki   I'm the massage.

Dodge   Oh. Good. Everything's ready.

Rikki *is surprised and fascinated by the state of the room.*

Dodge   I did explain to your boss.

Rikki   What?

Dodge   What's your name?

Rikki   Rikki.

Dodge   Where are you from?

Rikki   Upton Park.

Dodge   West Ham supporter?

Rikki   Yes.

Dodge   Never mind.

Rikki   Where do you want it? The massage, Mr Dodge. In here? In the bedroom?

Dodge   Not yet.

Rikki   I've only got half an hour.

Dodge   Have you eaten?

Rikki   Yes.

Dodge   When?

Rikki   Lunchtime.

Dodge   I want you to eat with me.

Rikki   Eat what?

Dodge   You'll see.

Rikki   You some sort of creep?

Dodge   Watch it!

Rikki   What do you want?

Dodge   I've done a meal. I want someone to share it. Right?

Rikki   Is that what you're paying for?

Dodge   That's between me and your boss.

Rikki   Know him, do you?

Dodge   Done business.

Rikki   I mean personally.

Dodge   Too many questions.

Rikki   Sorry.

Dodge   You staying or leaving?

Rikki   Staying.

Dodge   Sit down then.

Rikki   Here?

Dodge   Yes.

Rikki *sits at the table.*

Dodge (*tossing a box of matches at* **Rikki**)   Light the candles.

Rikki *lights the candles.*

Rikki   Where's the menu, Mr Dodge?

Dodge *goes into the kitchen to fetch the first course. As soon as he's out of the room,* **Rikki** *gets up and looks at* **Dodge***'s superb bicycle. He gets back to his seat before* **Dodge** *enters with two bowls of soup.*

Rikki   Tomato! My mum does that!

Rikki *starts to drink the soup.* **Dodge** *looks at him disapprovingly and offers* **Rikki** *a serviette.* **Rikki** *lays down his spoon, getting the message.*

Rikki   Sorry, Mr Dodge. Do you want me to say grace or something?

Dodge   That won't be necessary.

Rikki   You sound like a teacher at school. When he was on dinner duty, he used to say something in Latin or Greek . . . like he was casting a spell over the food. We used to call him Caligula . . . you know . . . after the video.

Dodge *picks up a sharp bread knife and starts to cut a slice of bread.*

Dodge   Bread?

Rikki   Just a bit.

Dodge *passes* **Rikki** *a slice on the point of the knife.*

Rikki   Sharp knife, Mr Dodge. Can I start? It's getting cold.

Dodge   Yes.

They both eat their soup.

Rikki   What's all this, then? Your birthday?

Dodge   Not mine.

Rikki   Someone else's?

Dodge   Do you have to ask questions?

Rikki   Sorry. Only asking, Mr Dodge.

Dodge   How old are you?

Rikki   Twenty-two . . . that's what I told the boss.

Dodge   Seventeen . . . sixteen . . . ?

Rikki   Leave off! I'm legal.

Dodge   Do you read?

Rikki   Books?

Dodge   Yes.

Rikki   No. Once read a book about sea fishing. I can read.

Dodge   Newspapers?

Rikki   Sometimes. Don't waste my money. I read other people's.

Dodge   Not interested in the news, then?

Rikki   You want to watch the telly?

Dodge   No I don't.

Rikki   Do what you want, Mr Dodge.

Dodge *clears away the soup plates and takes them to the kitchen. As soon as he has left the room,* **Rikki** *gets up and searches through the shelves above the workbench. He finds a pair of cyclist's gloves and pockets them. He also finds* **Dodge**'s *wallet, opens it and sees that* *there's about £70 in it. He hears* **Dodge** *coming back and stuffs the wallet back in its hiding place without taking any of the money. He sits down as* **Dodge** *enters with a covered dish and a plate of sausage rolls.*

Rikki   Great! Sausage rolls! Obviously a daring cook, Mr Dodge!

Dodge   Don't touch.

Dodge *goes to fetch the plates.* **Rikki** *immediately tries to lift the lid off the covered dish and burns his fingers.* **Dodge** *returns with the plates and starts to serve.*

Dodge   Two?

Rikki   Yes.

Dodge *passes* **Rikki** *the plate and, with a cloth, takes the lid off the covered dish.*

Rikki   Beans! Murder!

Rikki *takes a few spoonfuls of beans.*

Rikki (*singing*)   'Happy birthday to you . . . Happy birthday . . . '

Dodge (*silencing him*)   Thank you, Rikki!

Rikki   Sorry, Mr Dodge. Who is it, then?

Dodge   I'm not talking about it.

Rikki   Oh come on, sir!

Dodge   Why call me sir?

Rikki   Good manners, isn't it? You're like that, sir, aren't you? Go on, sir. Tell us, sir. Oh go on, sir.

Dodge   Just a kid I know.

Rikki   His birthday, is it?

Dodge   Yes.

Rikki   Your boyfriend, is he?

Dodge   Shut up!

Rikki   Only asking.

They carry on eating.

Your lover?

Dodge   I'm not gay.

Rikki   Bloody hell!

Dodge   You make so many assumptions.

Rikki   Oh God . . .

Dodge   You think we're all like you!

Rikki   Here! Leave me out of it, right? I'm doing my job, aren't I!

Dodge   He was my companion.

Rikki   Oh yes . . . I've heard of them.

Dodge   Just eat.

Rikki   Tell me if you want. I have to listen to all sorts of stuff.

Dodge   This is his favourite meal. He was supposed to be here.

Dodge *takes another mouthful of sausage roll.*

Rikki   *Bon appétit*, Mr Dodge.

Dodge   I didn't want to eat alone. Phoned the agency. Yours all right?

Rikki (*pushing his plate away*)   Memorable.

Dodge *takes the plates.* **Rikki** *gets up.*

Dodge   Sit down! There's more to come.

Rikki *looks at the half-built bicycle in the jig.*

Dodge *returns with some jelly out of a jelly mould.* **Rikki** *laughs when he sees what's next.*

Dodge   This is a bloody mistake.

Rikki   Looks OK to me.

Dodge *serves out some jelly onto* **Rikki**'s *plate.*

Rikki   Any cream?

Dodge *passes a jug of cream.* **Rikki** *helps himself.*

Dodge   I shouldn't have called you.

Rikki   Don't say that, Mr Dodge. I'm really enjoying this. Excellent jelly, Mr Dodge!

Rikki *eats the jelly with enthusiasm.*

Dodge   Why do you eat so fast?

Rikki   Brought up in a Children's Home. If you didn't eat fast you didn't get seconds.

Interested in football?

Dodge   I used to take Simon to see Chelsea.

Rikki   Chelsea!

Dodge   I suppose that was the start of it.

Rikki   Met him in the Shed?

Dodge   I knew him before that. I knew his mother.

Rikki   So he's called Simon, is he?

Dodge   Don't talk about him.

Rikki   What do you want to go to Chelsea for? They're a bunch of wimps!

Dodge   He wanted to go.

Rikki   Blimey! You've got problems there, mate! Did his mother come with you?

Dodge   Of course not.

Rikki   But you said you knew her. Shag me, love my son? That sort of game, was it?

Dodge *grabs the plates and takes them off into the kitchen.* **Rikki** *explores* **Simon**'s *toys.*

Dodge *returns with a birthday cake with the candles lit. There are only twelve candles on the cake.* **Dodge** *turns off the lights, although it is still* *light outside. He places the cake in front of* **Rikki** *on the table.* **Rikki** *is about to blow out the candles.*

Dodge Make a wish.

Rikki *makes a wish.*

Rikki Not telling you, mind.

Rikki *blows out all the candles and also the two other candles on the table for good measure.* **Dodge** *is irritated by this and he goes to turn on the light again.* **Rikki** *stares at the candles on the cake.*

Rikki Jesus! Twelve candles, Mr Dodge?

Dodge You can count too!

Rikki Your lover . . . sorry . . . companion . . . nice boy was he? Pretty? What a fucking mess!

Dodge Glass of orange?

Rikki Do us a favour!

Dodge *pours out a full glass of orange juice and plants it in front of* **Rikki**.

Dodge Drink it!

Rikki *sniffs it suspiciously, takes a sip, then downs the whole lot defiantly.*

Dodge Good boy.

Dodge *picks up the sharp knife and holds it in front of* **Rikki**.

Dodge Now cut the cake!

Rikki *doesn't move. He's worried by* **Dodge**'s *aggression.*

Dodge I said cut it!

Rikki *takes the knife and insolently removes the twelve candles from the cake before holding the knife poised above the cake.*

Dodge Make another wish!

Rikki *looks at the half-built bicycle and makes another wish. Then he cuts the cake roughly and deposits a slice on* **Dodge**'s *plate. He takes a small bit for himself and nibbles it.*

Dodge   Not bad, is it?

Rikki   Lovely.

Dodge   How long are you staying?

Rikki   Not long.

Dodge   Another twenty minutes?

Rikki   Can I phone the boss?

Dodge   Sure.

Rikki *goes to the phone and dials the agency.*

Rikki   Hi . . . Rikki . . . anything else tonight?
I'm still in Hammersmith.
Yes . . . OK . . . he's a food fetishist.
Where's that?
(*To* **Dodge**.) Pen? (**Dodge** *indicates where a biro and pad are kept.*)
OK . . . I got that. What time? Right.
You got this number?
Right.
Cash, credit card or account?
Cheers.
Bye . . .

Rikki *hangs up.*

Rikki   Got another job.

Dodge   Haven't had my time yet.

Rikki   Had the meal, haven't I?

Dodge   I'm paying for this.

Rikki   Offered you a massage.

Dodge   Stay a bit longer.

Rikki   Why?

Dodge   Company.

Rikki   Nothing queer.

Dodge   No.

Rikki   OK.

Dodge   Where's the next job?

Rikki   Not far. Round the corner.

Dodge   Finish your cake.

Rikki   No.

Dodge   OK was it?

Rikki   Lovely, Mr Dodge. Tell me about your bikes. Your shop, is it?

Dodge   Used to be. Gone out of business.

Rikki   Bust?

Dodge   More or less.

Rikki   Somebody screwed you?

Dodge   I'm a craftsman.

Rikki   Really?

Dodge   Halfords finished me. Flashy metal. That's where the money is.

Rikki   Start selling flashy metal.

Dodge   Can't make a living mending spokes. Got to sell bikes to survive.

Rikki   Custom-built stuff?

Dodge   You into bikes?

Rikki   Don't mind them.

Dodge   What have you got?

Rikki   A Raleigh. Too small for me now. Still use it sometimes. I used to love my bike. What's special about yours?

Dodge   (*indicating his own fast tourer that's hanging up*)   This one?

Rikki   Yes.

Dodge *fetches it down and places it in front of* **Rikki**.

Dodge Good frame. Reynolds 531 fork blades and stays. Butted frame tubes. Cyclone sealed bearing hubs. Suntour ARX derailler. Weinmann brakes. Campagnolo headset. Brilliant! [*Vary this description to suit the particular bicycle used in production.*] Built the wheels myself, of course.

Rikki Build wheels, do you?

Dodge Vital part.

Rikki (*while **Dodge** is replacing bike on its hanging frame*) Always had trouble with wheels. Out of shape. Ping! Another spoke gone. Used to fiddle on with one of them spoke key things.

Dodge Making matters worse.

Rikki Never could figure them out.

Dodge Off the peg jobs . . . some of the frames are OK. Lousy wheels. Get you out of the shop.

Rikki (*picking up one of **Dodge**'s wheels*) This one of yours?

Dodge Yes.

Rikki You built this from scratch?

Dodge Yes.

Rikki Really lasts, does it?

Dodge Yes.

Rikki Cost a bomb?

Dodge More to start with. Less in the long run.

Rikki What's the difference?

Dodge Quality parts. No one wants quality these days. A few enthusiasts, maybe. They do their own repairs when something happens. Get the parts off me. Don't blame them. That's what I'd do.

Rikki So what happened?

Dodge Got into a tangle with the VAT.

Rikki So you cut your losses and quit.

Dodge Craftsmanship doesn't pay. Trash rules.

Rikki Could you fix my bike?

Dodge Could do.

Rikki Selling off some of your wheels cheap?

Dodge Hold on.

Dodge *fetches a tape measure and measures* **Rikki**'s *inside leg.*

Dodge You need a 22-inch frame. [*This depends on the height of the actor.*] I might be able to help you.

Rikki I've got no money.

Dodge Liar.

Rikki Well, got some.

Dodge Stacks with what you're up to.

Rikki The boss collects the money. I just get a percentage. I live off tips, Mr Dodge. I'm doing all right.

Dodge You a good masseur?

Rikki Brilliant. Got magic fingers.

Dodge Practise on yourself, do you?

Rikki Shut your face. I'm trained. Qualified. I went on a government scheme. I'm a success story.

Dodge What sort of scheme's that, then?

Rikki I was your unemployed youth. They sent me to the swimming baths. They've got this Turkish suite, and this old geezer . . . all covered in tattoos and hairless . . . he did the massage. He showed me what to do and the punters liked being done by a young lad. When my time was up, they never kept me on. Said they were sorry, but they hadn't got the money. Saw this ad, for a masseur. Followed it up. Said I was twenty-two. Got the job, didn't I. Been at it for three months now. Have you got any of those sexy, one-piece racing outfits?

Dodge *rummages around in one of his boxes and finds one. He throws it over to* **Rikki**.

Rikki   Thanks, Mr Dodge!

Dodge   Tony.

Rikki (*putting away the suit in his shoulder bag*)   Tony. How did you get mixed up with this kid?

Dodge   Big mistake.

Rikki   You don't look the sort to me.

Dodge   What does 'the sort' look like?

Rikki   Not saying. Don't look like one, that's all.

Dodge   You know about these things, do you?

Rikki   Not saying.

Dodge   Ah . . .

Rikki   What happened?

Dodge   Met him and his mum in Benidorm. Me and his mum, we got on together. She's bright. Journalist. Freelance.

Rikki   You screw her?

Dodge   Shut it!

Rikki   Just asking. Get on with it. Go on!

Dodge   We got on together. Good couple of weeks. You been there?

Rikki   I haven't been anywhere. Except Southend.

Dodge   We got home, carried on. Used to see her two or three times a week. Used to cook for each other. You know . . . company. Simon was crackers on bikes. His mum used to park him here. Took him to the cinema. Bike trips. Camping.

Rikki   Great.

Dodge   Appeals to you, does it?

Rikki   Not half?

Dodge   We were away in Dorset.

Rikki   You and the kid.

Dodge   Yes. Weekend trip. Out all day. Really tired. Got the tent up. Cooked a meal.

Rikki   Beans!

Dodge   Got on great.

Rikki   Is that it?

Dodge   Just about.

Rikki   How old was he?

Dodge   Just a kid.

Rikki   Ten? Nine?

Dodge   Suppose so.

Rikki   Fucked him, did you?

Dodge *is enraged by this. He walks over to* **Rikki**'s *shoulder bag, picks it up and throws it at him.*

Dodge   Fuck off out of here!

Rikki   Fucked the kid! Is that it?

Dodge *grabs* **Rikki** *and tries to hustle him out of the door.* **Rikki** *surprises him with a hip throw and* **Dodge** *suddenly ends up on his back on the floor.*

Dodge   Jesus Christ!

Rikki   Neat!

Dodge   Fucking twat!

Rikki   Did judo at evening classes. Free with a UB40! Not bad, eh?

Dodge (*more stunned than injured*)   You've just broken my fucking back!

Rikki   Sorry, Mr Dodge . . . Tony . . . sir. Let's have a look.

As **Rikki** *tries to touch him,* **Dodge** *recoils, as though unwilling to be touched.*

Rikki   Steady. Let's see. It was a perfectly reasonable question. No need to fly off the handle. Sit still. That's better. I won't hurt you. Honest.

Dodge *calms down, but is still unwilling to be touched.*

Rikki   So there's you and this kid. Tell us, Tony. I want to know. Please.

Dodge   He just . . . kind of . . . flung his arms around me.

Rikki   Little Simon?

Dodge   . . . hung onto me as though I was the last driftwood in a big ocean. We never did anything really heavy together.

Rikki   What did you do?

Dodge   Ohhh . . . he just got curious about my body . . . about his . . . how things worked. All over in a moment. We . . .

Rikki   What?

Dodge   . . . we were lying there . . . him playing with me . . .

Rikki   . . . starkers . . .

Dodge   . . . and I just came off. Bang! That was that. Dodge the child-molester. Didn't seem such a big deal at the time.

Rikki   You OK?

Dodge   Yes. I think so. Fallen off the bike enough times.

Rikki   Thought you were an expert.

Dodge   Simon thought it was fantastic.

Rikki   A new toy. So what have you done with him?

Dodge   Last night his mother caught him playing with himself in the bath. They had a row. She's become jealous of me. My 'influence'.

Rikki   Still take her out?

Dodge   Not any more.

Rikki   Packed her in?

Dodge Got too involved. Too complicated. Didn't want to move in with them.

Rikki So you was screwing her and her son?

Dodge Wasn't like that exactly.

Rikki Has she found out?

Dodge I don't think so. I thought I'd give Simon a birthday treat. But she thumps her fist down and says 'No way!' He's got his own mates. You know . . . his own age. Always been his own boss as far as I was concerned.

Rikki This would look bad on the front page of the *News of the World*.

Dodge It would. It seemed natural at the time. A bit odd, really. But there we are.

Dodge *goes to the telephone.*

I've got to call him.

He dials.

Do you mind?

Rikki Go ahead.

Dodge Simon . . . Mum's out is she? Good. Yes, I'm sorry too.
Do you want to go camping with the scouts? Yes . . . you'll have a great time. Well . . . the bike'll be there when you get back.
Look . . . sorry it's been such a mess today. Happy birthday. Just do what she says. Give it time. Have you said anything? Good.
I'll be off on my trip.
Of course I'll send you a card. I'll send you loads!
Done your homework? Well get on with it! Watch the video later, then!
No, I won't tell her.
OK . . . sorry to interrupt.
'Bye.

Simon *has hung up on him.* **Dodge** *replaces the receiver.*

Rikki   What's the trip?

Dodge   I'm going to cycle round Britain.

Rikki   What, right round?

Dodge   Yes.

Rikki   Which way?

Dodge (*making a clockwise motion*)   That way.

Rikki (*imitating him*)   That way?

Dodge   Yes.

Rikki   Clockwise.

Dodge   Yes.

Rikki   Why?

Dodge   If I head northwards up the West coast, I'll have the wind behind me.

Rikki   You're mental.

Dodge   I've got to get away.

Rikki   Have you sold this place?

Dodge   I quit the lot next week.

Rikki   Where are you going to live?

Dodge   Going to store what's left of my stuff in a garage. Then off on my bike with my tent and get the hell out of it!

Rikki   Running away.

Dodge   Dead right.

Rikki   What from?

Dodge   This bloody city.

Rikki   It's OK.

Dodge   Owning things. Bills, income tax, VAT . . .

Dodge *scatters handfuls of letters, all unopened.*

Rikki   You're daft. You might have won the pools.

Dodge   Don't do them.

Rikki   No one ever writes to me.

Dodge   Somewhere out there, I'm filed on a dozen computers. I've got a shop so they think I've got money.

Rikki   So you'd rather be a tramp on wheels?

Dodge   While there's still some cash left.

Rikki *goes over to where* **Dodge**'s *wallet is hidden and fetches it out so that* **Dodge** *can see him.*

Rikki   If it'll make you feel better, you can give all your money to me.

Rikki *puts the wallet back again.*

Dodge   I'm not giving it away to anyone.

Rikki *is fascinated by* **Dodge**'s *brilliant bicycle.*

Dodge   Riding a bike's like flying. You know those dreams you sometimes have, when you kick your legs and take off? And you say: 'Look at me! Flying's easy! Come on! Just try it!' And you wonder why you haven't been picked for the Olympic games when you can clear a hundred metres at a single leap. When you're sailing down a long hill, and the bike is perfectly balanced and silent, and you look ahead, you might as well be flying under your own power. And you can hear and smell the countryside on a bike, and feel the pockets of warm and cold air sail past you as you go. There's nothing like it, Rikki.

Rikki   What are you going to live on? Hedgehogs?

Dodge   I'll manage.
So you were in a Children's Home?

Rikki   Yes. Till I was ten.

Dodge   What was that like?

Rikki   OK, I suppose. You don't know any different, do you . . . You think about having a mum and dad like normal kids at school, but then you have your treats, like going to the pantomime or the cinema. And you're there with all your mates. And you think kids with families are probably having hell kicked out of them. You're better off with what you know sometimes. I was adopted, mind. I've got a mum now.

Dodge   When did you get a mum?

Rikki   When I was ten. The people there, they got me all dressed up 'cause I was going to meet someone who wanted to adopt me. That's what the kids there dreamed of. Someone coming. Someone good . . . you know . . . to take you with them . . . to be your dad . . . take you on holidays and that . . . have your own room and your own things . . . possessions. Anyway, I was in this room and the door opened and this man and woman walked in, and I remember thinking, 'Bloody hell! I'm not going off with them! The other kids'll think I'm daft!' But I did. Just for the afternoon. You don't clear off for good, just like that. They have to get to know you, to see if they like you.

Dodge   Where did they take you?

Rikki   First time out?

Dodge   Yes.

Rikki   Caught the train to Southend. I'd been there before with the other kids . . . you know . . . from the Home. Seen the Waxworks. 'Torture through the Ages.' Not much cop. Supposed to be educational. Looked at the *Golden Hind*. Went on the racing cars by the pier. Great to be with someone with money to spend. When we was having a day out with the Home, we had to spend a lot of time just watching other kids having fun. Then we went to the Kursaal . . . big dippers and that. But we was running out of money. There was this incredible ride called the Toboggan. So Mum and Dad and me gets on this sledge thing and start to get hoisted up to the top of the Cresta Run. And once you're on it, there's no escape, even if you have a heart attack on the way up. 'Cause you can't see, when you pays your money, just how steep it is 'cause it goes right out of sight. But on the way up me Mum starts screaming and Dad's had a few drinks and says he feels sick and I was laughing. And when we gets to the top there's this lad with tattoos like a gipsy and he doesn't take the blindest notice of me Dad, who threatens to bottle him. And the next thing we know, we're charging down this vertical run on a wooden tray at a hundred miles an hour. And we all screamed our heads off. And when we got to the top of the next hump, Dad threw up and Mum lost her hat! And I thought, 'If they can do this for me, maybe they're not so daft.'

Dodge Still living with them?

Rikki Live with me mum.

Dodge What about your dad?

Rikki Dropped dead! In the front hall. Been on the booze. Boing! Dead!

Dodge When was that?

Rikki A few years back. Thought of killing him myself. Did it for me, didn't he!

Dodge What did you want to kill him for?

Rikki This and that.

Dodge Tell me.

Rikki No.

Dodge Private?

Rikki Yes.

Dodge What are your ambitions?

Rikki Me?

Dodge Yes.

Rikki Get some money. Get married. Have kids. Buy a Volvo. A place in Barking.

Dodge Is that it?

Rikki Yes.

Dodge I thought you weren't interested in girls.

Rikki Thought wrong, didn't you.

Dodge I suppose I did.

Rikki I do this massage job 'cause I like it and it makes me money. I love kids. I'm going to have a big family one day. And when I do, I'm going to love them. Going to play with them. Take them to the football. Trips to the seaside. See films together. Do something special at Christmas and birthdays. See these hands?

Dodge Yes.

Rikki There was a lot of hate in them once, but it's going away. They've handled so many bodies, you wouldn't believe it. Old ones, young ones, fat and skinny ones, queer and fucking queer! And it's made me strong. Look at my muscles! A lot of hate's gone out of me. Done me good, this job. My mum's proud of me. I buy her presents. Look after her.

Dodge Got a girl-friend?

Rikki Got a few.

Dodge Anyone special?

Rikki No. Got to find the right one for my kids, haven't I?

Dodge You'll have beautiful boys.

Rikki I think so. And if anyone gets their hands on them, I'll kill them.

Dodge I think you'd better go now.

Rikki What's the time?

Rikki *grabs* **Dodge***'s wrist and twists it to look at his watch.*

Rikki Still got a minute or two.

Dodge Do you want me to fix your bike, then?

Rikki Got enough bits?

Dodge Yes.

Rikki *(admiring the half-built bicycle)* I like travel. Fancy a trip to Southend?

Dodge   On the bikes?

Rikki   If you want.

Dodge   Better places to go than that.

Rikki   Is there?

Dodge   Too many cars.

Rikki   Where's Dorset? Is it far?

Dodge   Quite far.

Rikki   Is it good?

Dodge   Very good.

Rikki   What's there?

Dodge   Country. Cliffs. The sea. Better than Southend.

Rikki   Seen the sea.

Dodge   It's different. Depends where you go.

Rikki   Suppose so.

Dodge   What do you want to fix up?

Rikki   Are you stopping in tonight?

Dodge   Yes. Going to work on the bike.

Rikki (*gazing at the half-built bike*)   Reynolds 531?

Dodge   Yes.

Rikki   What size?

Dodge   22-inch frame. [*This size depends on the height of the actor playing* **Rikki**.]

Rikki   Got wheels, has it?

Dodge   They're in the shop.

Rikki   Look. I'm only going round the corner for the next 'un. Can I call back in on my way home?

Dodge   OK.

Rikki   Where's that racing outfit you give us? Oh yea, in the bag. This is going to make someone happy tonight! I'm wicked!

Dodge What do you mean 'wicked'?

Rikki Oh ... you know ... not really.

Dodge Am I wicked?

Rikki Definitely.

Dodge I don't think so.

Rikki Not all the time, maybe.

Dodge When?

Rikki Not when you're on the bike. With the kid you are.

Dodge It was an accident.

Rikki Not after the first time.

Dodge Who said it happened again?

Rikki 'Course it did! You done him, Mr Dodge. That's a fact. And you shouldn't of.

Dodge You know fuck all.

Rikki That's what you think.

Dodge He calls the tune.

Rikki He shouldn't.

Dodge Why?

Rikki You shouldn't let him.

Dodge Why?

Rikki You're grown-up. He isn't.

Dodge He is grown-up. In his way he is.

Rikki You were like his dad, with his mum and that. Dads shouldn't do things like that. Dads are for other things.

Dodge What do you know about it?

Rikki Plenty.

Dodge Like what?

Rikki Not saying.

Dodge Something happened to you? This Children's Home, queer was it?

Rikki   It was OK. It was good really. Saved my life. I think they did. Good people, Mr Dodge. Didn't agree with all of it. Too much God, not enough food. They weren't perfect. But they weren't bad either.

Dodge   Not quite what I asked.

Rikki   You was after dirty stories. I'm not telling none. Boys being boys is one thing. Grown-ups being boys is a pain in the arse! You don't need dirty stories from me. You've got your own, haven't you!

The bell in the front of the shop sounds.

Dodge   Hang on.

Jane *has walked through the shop to the back room and enters. She is carrying a shoulder bag of her own and a bag full of* **Dodge**'s *clothes that she has washed and ironed. She is surprised to see* **Rikki** *and wonders who he is.*

Jane   Oh! I didn't know you had company.

Rikki   Sorry.

Jane   Who's your friend?

Rikki   I'm just going, Mr Dodge.

Jane   Don't rush off just because I've come. Here are your things, Tony. (*To* **Rikki**.) I do all this for him. Crazy, don't you think?

Dodge   Thanks.

Jane   What's your name?

Rikki   I'm nobody.

Jane   Tell me.

Rikki   Rikki, Mrs . . .

Dodge   I think Rikki has another appointment.

Rikki   Yes.

Jane   Visiting are you?

Rikki   Got to dash!

Rikki goes to pick up his bag.

Jane   Wait! Oh look! All Simon's toys. And some of his books! That's where they got to! Well! I don't think you'll be needing these here any longer. Rikki, be an angel and carry this lot out to my car. Hold on! Where's a box? You don't mind me using one of yours, Tony?

She fetches one of **Tony**'s *boxes and empties out the contents. Then she holds the empty box in* **Rikki**'s *direction.* **Rikki** *doesn't move. He looks at* **Dodge** *for his approval.*

Rikki   Mr Dodge?

Dodge   Do what she says.

Rikki grabs the box from **Jane** *rudely, and starts to fill it with Simon's things.*

Jane   Is the skateboard mended yet? Simon was very anxious about that.

Dodge   Haven't had time.

Jane   Oh well! He'll have to go without!

Jane takes the skateboard out of the vice.

Rikki   Leave it, Mrs . . . It's no good with the wheels in bits. Tony'll mend it. He's clever, him.

Jane   I know. Do you want it? Take it.

Rikki   No! Look! He's good with wheels, aren't you, Tony.

Jane   What do you want to take things apart for? This was OK the last time I saw it.

Dodge   I was servicing the bearings.

Jane   It's just a toy, for God's sake!

Rikki takes the skateboard.

Rikki   You don't understand nothing! There's lots of little steel balls inside there. They get full of dirt and stuff so they

don't do their job proper. Clean them. Oil them. And they
don't half go! That's right, ain't it, Tony?

Dodge   Exactly right.

Jane is stuffing things into the box without paying much attention.
Rikki *is getting angry about this.*

Rikki   Oy! Mrs! Look at these!

Rikki *goes over to* **Dodge**'s *fast-touring bicycle that is hanging up, he
turns the pedal and sets the rear wheel spinning furiously.*

Rikki   Tony made them! Perfect! All them little balls doing
their job. One action and things are set spinning for ages.
That's my energy you're looking at. Still going, ain't it? Long
after what I've done. That machine, it's just waiting for
someone to make it come to life.

Rikki *goes to the box of toys while the wheel goes on spinning.*

Now where do you want me to stuff this?

Jane   By the shop door.

Rikki   Right, Mrs . . . Tony'll fix it . . . the skateboard!

Rikki *leaves with his bag and the box.*

Jane   OK. We've got to talk.

Dodge   Well?

Jane   Fetch me a coffee.

Dodge *walks off into the kitchen, shutting the door loudly.* **Jane**
*immediately gets a Walkman tape recorder out of her bag and sets it
going. She records herself.*

Jane   Tony Dodge's place . . . Wednesday 27th August . . .
(*She looks at her watch.*) . . . 6.47 pm . . .

*She then conceals the tape recorder, which is still recording, in her bag,
making sure that the built-in microphone will pick up the following
conversation. She sets it down on the table in front of her and awaits*
Dodge's *return with the coffee.*

[*Part Two may follow without an interval.*]

Part Two

Jane *is still sitting at the table as at the end of Part One.*

Dodge *brings in two cups of coffee. He sets them down on the table, where* **Jane** *is sitting, and moves her handbag out of the way.* **Jane** *conceals her concern about the new positioning of the tape recorder.* **Dodge** *sits with her at the table.*

Jane   Has Simon phoned?

Dodge   No.

Jane   Good.

Dodge   Thanks for doing these. (*Meaning the washing.*)

Jane   That's the last.

Dodge   Right.

Jane   When are you leaving?

Dodge   Next week. You know that.

Jane   Just making sure.

Dodge   Then you'll be rid of me.

Jane   Are you planning to write to Simon?

Dodge   Yes.

Jane   Don't.

Dodge   You can't stop me.

Jane   Don't try it.

Dodge   He's looking forward to postcards from all over the place. What's up with you, then? Two days ago you were all keen for this party. I get everything ready. Then 'He's not coming, you bastard. You'll never see him again!' And all that crap. What the hell's going on?

Jane   I went into the bathroom and he started screaming at me to get out. He's never done that before.

Dodge   Growing up, isn't he.

Jane   We were talking later and he tried to explain. You came up. I guessed the rest.

Dodge   Guessed what?

Jane   What have you done?

Dodge   Nothing.

Jane   I'm his mother. I've got a right to know the truth. There's no one else here. Just you and me. Now tell me.

Dodge   There's nothing to tell.

Jane   That won't do.

Dodge   You've dumped him on me for the past three years, while you fly about writing trashy stories . . .

Jane   Rubbish.

Dodge   All you've ever done is work out how to get him out of the way.

Jane   You think so?

Dodge   Yes.

Jane   You think bringing up a boy on your own is easy?

Dodge   No.

Jane   I have to earn money. I've got a good job. Unsocial hours. Of course there are problems when he's not at school. What am I supposed to do? Pack my job in?

Dodge   Possibly.

Jane   Thanks a lot.

Dodge   What did you do? You sent him round here. 'Go and see Tony.' 'Tony, can he come and have tea with you? I'm out on a job.' So I more or less adopt him.

Jane   You didn't mind.

Dodge   Of course I didn't. I love him. Great kid. And now you swing your bloody great axe on us! Talk about everything happening at once. I've lost everything now, haven't I. The shop's not your fault. For a year I was happy. So were you. Then . . . finish . . . go home . . . you're not staying. A week later . . . let's go to a film . . . come round for a meal . . .

Jane   What have you done to my son?

Dodge   Been like a father. You're jealous, aren't you! First it was 'Love me, love my son'. Now it's 'Hands off the pair of us!' But you're two separate people, aren't you? He's got his life, you've got yours.

Jane   I'll go to the police if I have to.

Dodge   What?

Jane   He's only twelve years old. I'm not bluffing. You've been at him, haven't you!

Dodge   What are you getting at?

Jane   You bloody well know!

Dodge   I'm the best friend he ever had.

Jane   Do you want the police round here?

Dodge   Of course not.

Jane   You've been screwing Simon.

Dodge   You're fucking mental!

Jane   I'll prove it. I'll take him to a doctor. No. The police will do that.

Dodge   How can you . . . ! To your own son!

Jane   Tell me now. Just the two of us.

Dodge   Have you any idea what would happen if you went to the police?

Jane   I mean it, Tony.

Dodge   And the social workers? Do you want everyone to find out how you've been neglecting him?

Jane   I haven't neglected him.

Dodge   You can't see it yourself, can you! You seem quite unable to see any fault in yourself. Let's start with the basics. You don't feed him properly. You don't wash his clothes often enough. You don't look after him like a mother should.

Jane   Of course I do.

Dodge   You wash my clothes, but you don't wash his! Who went to his school for parents' evenings? Not you! I did. You're always too busy or too tired. And they told me how Simon was being teased about being smelly!

Jane   You know perfectly well the clean clothes were there. He just never helped himself. Boys are like that.

Dodge   The social workers, they'll go to the school. They'll find out everything. You'll be amazed what they'll find out. If you go to the police, it'll end up with Simon being taken into care.

Jane   Nonsense.

Dodge   Like a bet? I'll lose him. And so will you! Jane, I beg you to believe me. There's no need to do anything rash. I haven't been screwing anyone. Certainly not Simon.

Jane   The doctor should be able to tell me.

Dodge   Are you seriously going to let some guy stick his fingers into Simon? Humiliate him? Just to satisfy some crazy idea of yours?

Jane   If you've given him some sort of disease, we need to know.

Dodge   Jesus Christ! I haven't done anything like that! It's all in your head!

Jane   What have you done?

Dodge   Pack it in!

Jane   You've put your arms round him. Cuddled him.

Dodge   Of course I have. You've seen us together. You never objected.

Jane I don't mean when I've been there. I mean when you go off camping. On holiday together. You've been very close, haven't you?

Dodge Yes.

Jane He's told me how you've cuddled him naked. How he's touched you.

Dodge Of course we undress. How do you suppose we keep clean? Look! What is this?

Jane Interested, isn't he?

Dodge What in?

Jane Things.

Dodge Normal kid.

Jane Used to be.

Dodge Christ!

Jane You just got carried away?

Dodge Shit!

Jane I can understand. Just tell me, Tony.

Dodge For fuck's sake!

Jane It isn't fair. After everything. Fucking tell me! OK . . . you've been naked together.

Dodge So what?

Jane He's told me, Tony. 'Mummy, he's all stiff down here.' How you've got him to wank you off! Let's both be adult about this, shall we? How often has this happened? Either you or him?

Dodge Shut your fucking face!

Jane Do you want me to bring Simon round here? I mean it! I will! I'll get him to repeat everything he's told me!

Dodge I don't believe you.

Jane Just try me! Let's get this out of the way now. Together. Privately.

Dodge Once.

Jane How often?

Dodge There was nothing bad about it. He was curious. Interested. You said so yourself. That's all there was to it.

Jane Did he suck you off?

Dodge Will you fuck off, you bloody woman! He was curious about what he had between his legs. Boys are like that!

Jane You know all about boys, do you?

Dodge I was a boy once, wasn't I? If he'd had his father around . . .

Jane . . . his father wouldn't have done that to him! I'm glad you've admitted it!

Dodge I'm not admitting anything!

Jane Too late!

Dodge If anyone's done him harm, it's you!

Jane Really?

Dodge . . . stopping him coming to his own birthday party! How's he supposed to understand what's going on in your sick mind? Don't try and make him feel guilty. He's a happy kid. What are you trying to do to him?

Jane If he'd been playing around with someone his own age, I wouldn't give a toss . . .

Dodge Oh? What's the difference?

Jane You're a bloody grown-up, aren't you! You should leave kids alone, shouldn't you?

Dodge I'm not into kids. You should know that, for Christ's sake! You've got a bloody short memory, you know that? Look! Simon started it . . .

Jane For God's sake!

Dodge . . . he wanted it! I just didn't say no! It was all over in seconds. You know how fast I come sometimes. There's no point in making a song and dance about it years after the event!

Jane   Years?

Dodge   When do you think this all happened?

Jane   Jesus! How many others have there been?

Dodge   What others?

Jane   Other children.

Dodge   None! Of course there haven't. There aren't going to be any either.

Jane   How do you know?

Dodge   Because I know! It was a one-off. Anyway, you can't talk about what's good and what isn't.

Jane   Why?

Dodge   All those books you let him read. And the videos.

Jane   What books?

Dodge   The first time we went off into the country, the poor kid was struggling along with a great, fat book about the Manson murders!

Jane   *Helter Skelter*?

Dodge   Yes. Great stuff for a kid. Rape, mass murder, torture . . .

Jane   He can read what he likes.

Dodge   Yes! I know! And the videos. Good way of shutting him up, is it? Drugs, orgies and mutilation? I suppose you just call that educational?

Jane   I don't know what he gets from the video shop.

Dodge   Well, you ought to! You're his mother!

Jane   I never tried to stop him watching what he wanted. Books, films . . . it's up to him.

Dodge   Exactly! And all he's done is go from what he's seen on your television into real life. Lucky it was only sex he was interested in! He might have wanted to cut me up! You know what you taught him? Sex is cruel, without feeling, something you take when you need it!

Jane   What are you talking about? He's just a boy.

Dodge   You actually think he's too young to think like that, don't you! The truth is, you let him grow up too fast. While you were fighting with your husband, Simon was left to fend for himself, like a mongrel on a rubbish tip!

Jane   I had to fight tooth and nail to keep my home together. Of course Simon suffered. I know that. But I won custody, thank God. And I've rebuilt our home together. And I don't need you to give me lectures about the price we both had to pay.

Dodge   I apologise. I don't want to lecture you. Simon wasn't the innocent little boy you seem to think he was. By the time he met me, he was desperate to find someone to cling to. He was all tangled up inside.

Jane   What exactly do you mean?

Dodge   I mean boys don't tell their mothers everything. In my way, however imperfectly, I've tried to teach him about love, affection, caring for someone . . .

There is a mechanical click from the tape recorder.

Dodge   What was that?

Jane   What?

Dodge *goes over to* **Jane**'s *bag and searches it. He finds the tape recorder.*

Dodge   Christ!

Jane   Give me that!

Dodge *takes out the tape cassette.*

Dodge   You filthy fucking bitch!

She tries to grab it from him but he smashes it open and the tape unspools as he tries to rip it to bits.

Dodge   Fuck you! Fuck you! (*Holding up the tape.*) I suppose you get used to playing this sort of trick in your business? All part of a day's work?

Jane   I don't want to hear from you ever again. If you attempt to contact Simon, I'll go straight to the police. Do you understand?

Jane *storms out, leaving the door open.*

Dodge, *in a state of shock, starts to gather up the bits of tape cassette and the torn recording tape. He is unsure how to dispose of the evidence. As he is hiding the bits in one of the boxes, the outer doorbell rings. He turns and a child's yellow and blue BMX wheel rolls through the door and lands at his feet.*

Rikki *enters.*

Rikki   It's me! Can I make a phone call?

Dodge *beckons him in to do what he wants.* **Rikki** *goes to the phone and dials his agency.*

Rikki   Hello? Rikki. Hammersmith still. No, I've finished for the night. You never warned me that cunt was into water sports! (*Aside to* **Dodge**.) He wanted to piss on me!
You did know! He told me the other guy you sent played. I don't know. Jimmy, or Alex, maybe? I thumped him. Twice. Once in the belly and once with my knee on the way down. He got heavy with me! I was being reasonable! I'm not doing nothing I don't want to do. No. He wasn't pleased. He said sorry. He liked being hit! Yes. I'll come round tomorrow. Pick my money up, right?

Rikki *replaces the receiver.*

Got all your problems sorted out, then? Feeling sorry for yourself?

Rikki *approaches* **Dodge** *cautiously.* **Dodge** *recoils each time* **Rikki** *tries to touch him.* **Rikki** *has to coax* **Dodge** *into trusting him to massage his temples and the sides of his face.*

Rikki   Easy. Easy now. Come on. It's only me. That's better. Lay your head back. That's it. They like this. Calms

most of them down. You know. Rikki says Relax! Blimey!
You're shaking. What's she done to you?

Dodge   Nothing.

Rikki   Do you ever tell the truth?

Dodge   Of course I do.

Rikki   . . . he lied . . . Seen the last of her?

Dodge   I hope so.

Rikki   Is that better?

Dodge   Ummm.

Rikki   What about this bike? Like to get my leg over. Try it
for size. Where are the wheels, then?

Dodge   Next door.

Rikki   I'll get them.

Rikki *goes to look for the wheels next door.*

Dodge   Behind the boxes.

Rikki (*off*)   Where?

Dodge   By the wheel jig.

Rikki   Got them!

Rikki *comes back with a front and back wheel, each beautifully made.*

These are wicked! You make them?

Dodge   Yes.

Dodge *fetches out the bicycle frame, which is set on its own free-standing jig.* **Rikki** *passes him the back wheel.* **Dodge** *slips it on, using quick release hubs.* **Rikki** *passes him the front wheel and* **Dodge** *puts that on. He fetches a frame pump from one of the workbenches and passes it to* **Rikki**.

Dodge   Give the back one plenty of air.

Rikki *pumps the rear tyre busily.*

Rikki   You'll never guess what I've got on underneath this
lot! Is that enough?

Dodge Yes.

Rikki *replaces the valve cap and passes the pump to* **Dodge**. *While* **Dodge** *is putting the pump back,* **Rikki** *slips out of his clothes to reveal the one-piece racing suit that he has on underneath. He shows himself off to* **Dodge**.

Rikki Well! Is it me?

Dodge *releases the bike from the jig.* **Rikki** *picks it up off the jig and holds it up above his head and turns round a couple of times.*

Rikki Blimey! It's as light as a feather!

He sets the bike down and **Dodge**, *standing at the front of the bike, with the front wheel between his knees and the handlebars firmly in his hands, beckons* **Rikki** *to get on.* **Rikki** *mounts the bike nimbly while* **Dodge** *holds it upright.*

Dodge How does that feel?

Rikki Fantastic!

Dodge Imagine the sun shining on your back. There's no traffic. Mile after mile is passing by and you're feeling strong and full of energy. Some trees are overhanging the road. Watch out for a load of insects! You have to squint to stop them getting in your eyes. As soon as you're out in the sunlight again, they're gone.

Rikki Good!

Dodge Then you pass some banks covered in meadowsweet. There's a lovely smell. Enough to make you drunk!

Rikki *sniffs deeply.*

Dodge There's a farm ahead! The road is covered in mud and cow dung. You have to slow down a bit. Try to find a clean path through it all. Farmyard smells!

Rikki Poo!

Dodge There's a wood fire burning in the house. Wood smoke! Then you're past and away. And you start to fly down a long, straight hill!

Rikki   Weee!

Dodge *leans forward and kisses the top of* **Rikki**'s *head.*

Rikki *leaps off the seat and throws his arms around* **Dodge** *and hugs him.*

Rikki   How much is it worth?

Dodge   £350 to you. A bargain.

Rikki   Bloody hell!

Rikki *stops hugging* **Dodge** *and wheels the bicycle away.*

Rikki   I think I'll stick to nicking them!

Rikki *rests the bicycle up against the table and admires it.*

Dodge   Do you want to ride it?

Rikki   Yes! Can we go off for the day?

Dodge   Where would you like to go?

Rikki   Anywhere.

Dodge   Let's go west. I've got some great routes. Off the main roads, mostly.

Rikki   OK.

Dodge   Are you serious?

Rikki   Yes.

Dodge   You wouldn't last thirty miles.

Rikki   I would! Let's go tomorrow and I'll prove it!

Dodge   Tell you what! Tomorrow we'll go off on a shorter run. Twenty miles or so. Check out the bikes.

Rikki   OK.

Dodge   See how that goes.

Rikki   Got to fetch my money in the morning. They owe us quite a bit. Let's go in the afternoon.

Dodge   Come here for two o'clock.

Rikki   Right! Had a job finding out how to get into this! (*Meaning the one-piece racing suit.*) Drove the other guy wild! He said I'd have to shave my legs. Why do they do that? Does it make you go faster?

Dodge   Lessening the wind resistance?

Rikki   Wouldn't make that much difference, would it?

Dodge   If you fall off and have to have bandages stuck all over, you can pull them off again without pulling your hairs out.

Rikki   Is that it?

Dodge   Vanity too.

Rikki   Do you shave yours? Let's have a look.

Rikki *lifts up* **Dodge***'s tracksuit bottoms to have a look.*

Dodge   Used to. Haven't bothered lately.

Rikki   You haven't had your massage yet.

Dodge   Oh God! Do I have to?

Rikki   'Course you do! Take your clothes off!

Rikki *fetches his bag and starts to lay out his things for business. He produces a large towel, which he flaps before laying it out on the floor. A small cloud of talc flies into the air. He sets a cushion at one end of the towel. He gets out various talcs, oils, intensive-care creams, deodorants and finally a soft toilet roll.* **Dodge** *has been watching this performance without undressing.*

Rikki   Come on!

Rikki *goes over and takes him by the hand and drags him to his feet.* **Dodge** *takes off his tracksuit and top. He is left wearing his Y-fronts.*

Dodge   Which way up?

Rikki   On your belly.

Dodge *tries to make himself comfortable on the floor with the cushion.* **Rikki** *puts talc on his hands and rubs it in. He then takes a spray-on deodorant and sprays it on* **Dodge***'s feet and under his armpits.* **Rikki**

then takes the talc and sprinkles it all over **Dodge**'s *back. He kneels down and starts the massage. After a while,* **Dodge** *speaks.*

Dodge   You think you're going to get a new bike out of this!

Rikki   Shut your face!

Dodge   Well you're not!

Rikki *carries on with his work.*

Rikki   I've always wanted an older man in my life, Tony. You know. Someone to look up to, show me things. Take me out. Not all the time. Just occasionally. You know? I don't want someone gay. Never leave you alone. Well . . . probably not gay . . . wouldn't mind . . . as long as it was safe. Personally, I'm a safe-sex stud. That's what I call myself. You listening?

Dodge   Ummm . . .

Rikki   Tony . . .

Dodge   Umm?

Rikki   You know I was telling you about my father.

Dodge   Umm.

Rikki   There's other things too. I had my own room, you know. For the first time. I'd always slept in a dormitory with the other boys at the Home. It took some getting used to. Being on my own and that. I'd been with my new parents for about a year. Really settled in. Then, one night, my dad came into my bedroom and started chatting and that. And then he kind of slipped his hand into my pyjamas and started playing with my cock. I was dead embarrassed. I just kind of froze. I wasn't exactly innocent. Not after all those years in the Home. But I wasn't expecting that from my dad. He used to do all sorts to me. He went down on me. He never tried to get inside, thank God. I think my mum guessed, but I never said anything. She was scared of him. Sometimes he'd have a drinking party with his mates. One of them used to come up to my room. I think Dad must have told him. And he used to put fifty pence by my bedside and then go down on me. I used to

let him. God knows what he got out of it. My cock must have
stuck up like . . . like . . .

Dodge   A small white thumb.

Rikki   Small white thumb? I suppose it did. How did you
know that, then? From your Simon? Christ! You're not really
into kids, are you?

Dodge   Don't you start.

Rikki   You're not, are you?

Dodge   No.

Rikki   Honest?

Dodge   Honest.

Rikki   That's good. Chaos here.

Rikki *starts playing with some of the unopened letters.*

I've always loved getting letters. No one ever used to write to
me at the Home. When my birthday came round I used to
hope that something would come in the post. It never did. Got
cards from the other kids. We did that for each other. Not the
same as the postman bringing you something. From outside. I
used to think they knew where I was. My real parents. Like
they were testing me. To see if I really loved them. I thought
they'd come one day and take me away. Maybe they'd write
to me. Tell me they hadn't forgotten me.

Rikki *starts to open a brown envelope.*

Bike mag . . . You know I said I wanted to get married and
that?

Dodge   You haven't finished the massage.

Rikki   . . . have kids and that . . . Well, you know in films
and on the telly and that . . . stories . . . you know . . . kids kind
of fall in love with one another, don't they. I know it sounds
daft. Well . . . it doesn't happen. Not to me. Never been in love
with anyone. Not like you're supposed to. Just sex. Bodies.
Coming off. Together. Alone. It's dead. If it was ever in me. I

don't love anyone. I don't know how. I'm different. They done it to me. That's what I think.

Rikki *opens another large envelope. Inside he finds a collection of photographs of little boys.*

Rikki   What's this, then?

Dodge   Christ!

Rikki   Who are all these little kids?

Dodge   I don't know. Give me that.

Rikki   What do you do with these then?

Dodge   I didn't know they were there.

Rikki   You said you wasn't into kids. You fucking liar!

Dodge   I don't know where they came from.

Rikki *throws the photos at* **Dodge**, *who tries to pick them up.* **Rikki** *goes over to the piles of boxes in a fury.*

Rikki   What else have you got hidden away?

Dodge   Nothing. Look! Leave my stuff alone!

Rikki *finds a box with more photos and magazines of naked boys. He picks one up and waves it in* **Dodge**'s *face.*

Rikki   Fucking hell! Look at this! Look at this!

Rikki *empties the box over* **Dodge**'s *head.*

Rikki   You said Simon was a one-off! You fucking liar!

Dodge *slaps* **Rikki**'s *face.*

Rikki   Don't you fucking hit me!

Rikki *hurls himself at* **Dodge**, *who parries a couple of punches before throwing* **Rikki** *across the room.* **Rikki** *is very distressed and gets dressed as quickly as he can.*

Rikki   Stick them in the oven, do you? Turn them into gingerbread? Little kids who've lost their way?

Dodge   Take the bike! Take it!

Rikki   Fuck the bike!

Dodge   You can have it. I'm sorry.

Rikki   You tricked me. That's it! Finished!

Dodge   It's not like you think.

Rikki   Shit!

Dodge   Why don't you listen?

Rikki   You think you can talk yourself out of any bloody corner. I know, see? I know what happens!

Dodge   I'm sorry about what happened to you. That wasn't me.

Rikki   Whose kids are these, then? What do you do? Wank over them?

Dodge   I don't know.

Rikki   'Course you do! There's no one in the world you can trust! Just men after your body!

Dodge   I can help you, Rikki.

Rikki   Like shit!

Dodge   Take the bike. Try it out.

Rikki   I wanted someone to talk to. Someone to listen.

Dodge *gathers up* **Rikki**'s *things and stuffs them in his bag.*

Dodge   Please go now.

Dodge *tosses* **Rikki** *his bag.* **Rikki** *picks it up and reaches into a side pocket.*

Rikki   You deserve cutting up! You know that!

Dodge   Fuck off!

Rikki *suddenly pulls a knife out of the side pocket of the bag and holds it at* **Dodge**'s *throat. He forces* **Dodge** *onto the floor.*

Rikki   Look at you! You daft shit! Fuck little kids, would you? What with? What with, Mr Dodge? Someone ought to cut it off and stuff it down your lying throat!

Dodge *is terrified on the floor.* **Rikki** *leaves him and goes over to the wallet and takes all the money.*

Rikki   What have you done, then? Followed kids around the park? Watched them coming out of school? Pocket full of sweets, Mr Dodge? Get dressed, you look horrible!

Dodge *goes towards* **Rikki** *who is going through the wallet.* **Rikki** *sticks his knife out.*

Rikki   Yea? Yea? Back off!

Dodge   It's not like that. You've got it wrong. I don't do anything like that.

Rikki   Oh yes?

Dodge   I'm not a danger to anyone.

Rikki *has found a photo of Simon in the wallet. He holds it out. When* **Dodge** *comes close to take it.* **Rikki** *throws it at him scornfully.* **Dodge** *picks it up.*

Dodge   Who says it's not natural, Simon and me? He's entitled to his own body, his emotions, his feelings. You ought to know that, for Christ's sake! If Simon wants me . . . It's important to him! I am! I'm part of his life! There are plenty of kids like Simon who need a mate. That's what I was. We were good for one another and balls to anyone who says we weren't! It may be finished. I think it probably is finished. But we didn't get our sums wrong!

Rikki   Bollocks!

Dodge   Whatever they say. Whatever you think! You think you're very smart. Know everything, don't you! Well you ought to know something after what's happened to you! All you do is go crazy! Waving that fucking knife around! Scaring the shit out of me!

Rikki   Good!

Dodge   Mr UB40! Judo champ! Mr Magic Fingers! I cared for him. I loved him. He wasn't getting it from her. From anyone else . . . You know something? I met you ten years too late.

Rikki   Ten years too late?

Dodge   I'd have done you good.

Rikki   Done me good and proper! Climbing up the stairs with fifty pence in your hand.

Dodge   Not like that. Don't blame me for what they did. That wasn't me.

Rikki   Never is you!

Dodge   I'd have given you what you were looking for.

Rikki   What was that?

Dodge   Taken you out on trips. Cared for you. Fed you. Cleaned you up.

Rikki   My mum done that for me.

Dodge   I'd have treated you well. Honest. I would.

Rikki   I know why! You'd have got at me. Little by little. Being nice and that. Getting me where you wanted. Cleaned me up, would you? In and out of the bathroom? No thanks. I could do that for myself, Mr Dodge.

Dodge   Sure. Of course you could.

Rikki   And all the time you'd be waiting for your chance to get in! Hopping around like a spider! A treat. A trip. A present. Ever so nice! At least those guys with their money didn't promise one thing and take another. They did come to the point, Mr Dodge. More honest than you'll ever be. It was simple. Just trade. No emotions. No feelings. Me selling. Them buying. Business. A good start, having some money in your pocket.

Dodge   Exactly what I'm getting away from.

Rikki   This crazy trip of yours. What are you going to do when it's finished? Go round again in the other direction?

Rikki *whirls his hand round in an anti-clockwise direction.*

This way?

Dodge   I don't know.

Rikki You were lucky. Just now you were. Something inside me wanted to cut you up!

Dodge Why didn't you?

Rikki I'm not really into murder. If I was, you'd be done by now good and proper. Close thing. You want to be careful, Mr Dodge. You could get yourself into trouble!

Dodge I'm ashamed of all this. (*Meaning the child pornography.*) I am. I wanted to find out what was going on inside me. I didn't know how to get rid of it. Couldn't put it in the bin. Someone might find it. Thought about burning it. Someone might see. I was going to put it in someone else's bin. Thought someone might catch me. I used to wish Jane and me would get back together again. Not any more! Maybe someone else will turn up. I'm not interested in men, Rikki. I wish I was sometimes. Might make things easier. I've played with the idea. Escort agencies. The odd masseur. Just playing games. Doesn't work for me. Then Simon comes back into my life, bouncing into the shop, excited, full of his chatter. He throws himself at me. Jumps on my lap with his comics. I have to read to him. *Bash Street Kids*. *Wizzer and Chips*. *Spiderman*. He's really made me love him. He worked at it night and day. He picked me out, Rikki. I never went after him. He chose me. He honoured me.

Rikki Don't make me sick!

Dodge I couldn't refuse him, Rikki. Why do people hate me for loving him? What do they know? Now I've lost almost everything. They'd wipe me out if they could. I'm surprised at you, though. I didn't expect that from you.

Rikki You're full of shit, Mr Dodge. You think you're doing good with little Simon. People who've done things never think they're the ones who've done wrong. It's everyone else, but not them! Truth is, you were good for Simon if you hadn't done what you done. It's as simple as that, Mr Dodge.

Dodge Should I phone him?

Rikki   Leave him alone. Let him phone you, if he wants.
Don't pester him. Don't stir it up. Let it settle. He'll find his
own bunch of mates. If he's the way I think he is, he won't
cause no trouble. Maybe sting you for a few quid when he's
short.

Dodge   You reckon?

Rikki   I know about these things. Had to, didn't I! It'll cost
you, mind.

Dodge   Will it?

Rikki   Advice. My knowledge.

Rikki *takes the bicycle and wheels it over to the door.*

You did say I could have this, didn't you?

Dodge *waves his hand as though to say 'Take it. I don't give a damn
any more!'*

Rikki   I have paid for it. In my way I have.

Dodge   If that's what you want to believe.

Rikki   See the rest of the world on this beautiful machine!
Right? Mr Dodge. Tony. Sir.

Rikki *collects the rest of his things and leaves with the bicycle.*

Methuen Modern Plays

include work by

Jean Anouilh
John Arden
Margaretta D'Arcy
Peter Barnes
Sebastian Barry
Brendan Behan
Edward Bond
Bertolt Brecht
Howard Brenton
Simon Burke
Jim Cartwright
Caryl Churchill
Noël Coward
Sarah Daniels
Nick Dear
Shelagh Delaney
David Edgar
Dario Fo
Michael Frayn
John Godber
Paul Godfrey
David Greig
John Guare
Peter Handke
Jonathan Harvey
Iain Heggie
Declan Hughes
Terry Johnson
Sarah Kane
Charlotte Keatley
Barrie Keeffe
Robert Lepage
Stephen Lowe

Doug Lucie
Martin McDonagh
John McGrath
David Mamet
Patrick Marber
Arthur Miller
Mtwa, Ngema & Simon
Tom Murphy
Phyllis Nagy
Peter Nichols
Joseph O'Connor
Joe Orton
Louise Page
Joe Penhall
Luigi Pirandello
Stephen Poliakoff
Franca Rame
Mark Ravenhill
Philip Ridley
Reginald Rose
David Rudkin
Willy Russell
Jean-Paul Sartre
Sam Shepard
Wole Soyinka
C. P. Taylor
Theatre de Complicite
Theatre Workshop
Sue Townsend
Judy Upton
Timberlake Wertenbaker
Victoria Wood

Methuen Student Editions

For a Complete Catalogue of Methuen Drama titles
write to:

Methuen Drama
Random House
20 Vauxhall Bridge Road
London SW1V 2SA